WORRY-FREE
FAMILY FINANCES

WORRY-FREE
FAMILY FINANCES

*Three Steps to Building and
Maintaining Your Family's
Financial Well-Being*

Bill and Mary Staton

McGRAW-HILL

NEW YORK   CHICAGO   SAN FRANCISCO   LISBON   LONDON
MADRID   MEXICO CITY   MILAN   NEW DELHI   SAN JUAN
SEOUL   SINGAPORE   SYDNEY   TORONTO

The *McGraw·Hill* Companies

Library of Congress Cataloging-in-Publication Data

Staton, Bill.
 Worry-free family finances : three steps to building and maintaining
your family's financial well-being / by Bill Staton and Mary Staton.
  p. cm.
  ISBN 0-07-140984-X (pbk. : alk. paper)
  1. Finance, Personal—United States. 2. Investments—United States.
I. Staton, Mary. II. Title.
HG179.S812 2003
332.024—dc21

                                                           2003013007

1 2 3 4 5 6 7 8 9 0   DOC/DOC   0 9 8 7 6 5 4 3

ISBN 0-07-140984-X

This publication is designed to provide accurate and authoritative information in regard
to the subject matter covered. It is sold with the understanding that neither the author
nor the publisher is engaged in rendering legal, accounting, or other professional service.
If legal advice or other expert assistance is required, the services of a competent professional person should be sought.
                    —*From a declaration of principles jointly adopted by a committee of the*
                                 American Bar Association and a committee of publishers.

 This book is printed on recycled, acid-free paper containing a minimum of 50%
recycled de-inked fiber.

McGraw-Hill books are available at special quantity discounts to use as premiums and
sales promotions, or for use in corporate training programs. For more information, please
write to the Director of Special Sales, Professional Publishing, McGraw-Hill, Two Penn
Plaza, New York, NY 10121-2298. Or contact your local bookstore.

Contents

WORRY-FREE
FAMILY FINANCES

1

Welcome!

Everybody gets so much information all day
long that they lose their common sense.
—GERTRUDE STEIN

Welcome to what we believe is a simple, easy-to-use text that will enable you as a family to manage your personal finances in a lot less time and with a lot less worry and risk and have a ton of fun doing it.

This is not the be-all and end-all of financial books. If there were such a thing, it would be an encyclopedia unto itself. Booksellers offer thousands of titles about investing, managing money, mutual funds, retirement plans, women and money, men and money, children and money, long-term health care, estate planning, and so on. The list seems almost endless and is growing rapidly. In addition, there are dozens of financial publications with different emphases, alongside an Internet stuffed with financial information (and lots of misinformation too). No one, including us, can possibly keep up with it, and we do not try. Neither should you.

Money appears to be a confusing subject, but it doesn't have to be and ought not to be when it is explained in plain English, which we have done within these pages. We designed *Worry-Free Family Finances* to build your and your family's foundation for managing your money easily and profitably, to help you design your own blueprint for monetary success. As we all know, it's impossible to construct a home or a building without a well-designed blueprint, and that is surely the case with money as well.

There is a certain Buddhistic calm that comes from having money in the bank.
TOM ROBBINS

What we offer is what people, particularly families, really need and desire: simple steps to modify their financial-behavior patterns—one at a time in digestible bites—to get on the road to financial well-being and, yes, even to become millionaires. If we've done our job, we'll motivate you to seize the initiative and gain control over your financial life in an easy yet profound way.

We offer significant credentials and experience. Bill has been an investment adviser/money manager for 33 years, while Mary has been his business partner for the last 8 years. Together we have helped more than 100,000 people across the United States and in 12 foreign countries take control of their financial futures. Our concepts for achieving wealth are time-proven and have empowered people from all walks of life. As this is a family-oriented investment book, we show adults and children alike that they can establish and reach their financial dreams without the use of outside advisers or managers simply by investing as little as $50 a month. We show them how to make the most of their money with the least risk and in the shortest time. Our strategies work for anyone, regardless of gender, age, or income, who wishes to seize the fantastic opportunities the American free-enterprise system offers.

We also offer a perspective few readers have heard before. For example, we believe that no one should ever buy a mutual fund. Ever!

Worry-Free Family Finances is designed to answer the money questions of you and your family, who are busier and have less time to think about money than ever before. It illuminates the phenomenal opportunities that exist within the American system and shows how you can achieve above-average returns with virtually no risk in about one hour a year, completely eliminate the use of a stockbroker, and cut taxes, investment expenses, and commissions to virtually zero.

We have developed a national reputation for making a complex subject simple by explaining it in everyday language that is so simple that even first- and second-graders can understand at least parts of it. Our son Will got started on his own market-beating portfolio on the way to Sunday school when he was seven. Today his net worth is greater than the average family's.

No, we don't know all the answers. No one does. Yes, we have made mistakes individually, as a couple, and also with our blended family (two children each). That's a real advantage for you because now we know many things you shouldn't do when it comes to personal and family finances. Once you learn what not to do, it becomes much easier to discover what you should do.

Worry-Free Family Finances provides a new angle on money and investing in part because it is written by a married couple. Study after study shows that one of the key divisive points in male-female relationships is money, specifically the different approaches to personal finance taken by men and women.

We've overcome this divisiveness in our relationship and can demonstrate to others how to achieve common ground on money and personal finances. Since we approach the issue of money from the male and female perspectives simultaneously, every reader will be able to relate to one if not both of us. We have used our own advice with our four children, starting Bill's two children on investing when they were born and helping Mary's two children with investment plans when Bill and Mary got married.

Nobody cares more about your money than you do. The government certainly won't take care of you (do you really believe in the health of

Every morning I get up and look through the Forbes list of the richest people in America. If I'm not there, I go to work.

ROBERT ORBEN

Social Security?); many companies won't do much, if anything, for you; you won't win the lottery even though you may dream about it; and your children might take care of you, but would you want them to? There's no one left to take care of you financially but you. The earlier you start taking care of yourself, the better off you'll be.

Worry-Free Family Finances will show you in clear, easy-to-follow logical steps how to be your own successful money manager and how to make the most of your and your family's money with least risk in the least personal time. You and your family will discover how simple it is to develop a program to get you where you need to be financially by the time you need to be there.

MONEY IS TOO IMPORTANT TO TAKE TOO SERIOUSLY

Far too many money books treat money much too seriously. We treat money seriously too, but not deathly seriously. Just as life should be fun, money should be fun too, and for the entire family, because money is an important part of life but not the only part. For all of you who want to make money simple and fun and have an uncomplicated plan for financial action, *Worry-Free Family Finances* is for you.

We've read dozens and dozens of financial tomes in our 40 + years of experience. Many are "cafeteria" books that tell you all the alternatives (like describing food in a cafeteria line) but don't help you sort out what's best for you (how to eat right) and your family. They usually fail to speak to young people at all.

There are three sides to building wealth, a triangle if you will, or even better, a pyramid with a solid foundation:

1. Save more
2. Give more
3. Invest wisely

That's how this book is organized. No, we won't show you how to earn more money in your current career or profession. But if you follow our basic formula, you can achieve financial dreams well beyond what you ever imagined. Here it is:

100 percent of your monthly after-tax income
Less: money invested wisely for your family's financial future
Less: money to give to causes and organizations you want
to support
Less: money to have fun
= money to pay all other expenses

The bulk of financial publications are devoted to telling you how to invest your money, and there are usually the same quotes, such as "pay yourself first" and "put all the money you can into a retirement plan." There is certainly nothing wrong with this advice, except that it is what links other financial books together, making them look pretty much the same.

THE THREE STEPS

"Save more" describes an easy, creative way to find out where the leaks are in your financial ship and how to plug them. It also gives you a number of ways to reduce spending, including a section called "Do You Really Need an Expensive Wedding?" and another called "Buying a Car the Right Way."

"Give more" includes a number of inspiring stories from the famous and the nonfamous alike on how giving away money not only has been uplifting in their personal lives but also has created enormous amounts of personal wealth. It's easy to be a giver when there's plenty of money to give, but we believe that the size of a gift is measured by how much is left over. Many givers, including ourselves, have kept up their giving and even increased it regularly even when times were tough.

"Invest wisely" outlines our "one-hour-a-year" approach to beating 75 to 85 percent of all investment professionals 100 percent of the time. We debunk the widespread myth that owning stock mutual funds is the best way to invest.

Some financial books analyze the constant shifts taking place in financial markets. Others endorse cookie-cutter solutions offered by the financial-services industry as "the way" to achieve financial stability. Still others, and there have been several best-sellers among them in recent years, encourage people to change their financial "attitudes" so that their financial "behavior" will improve. We disagree.

By demystifying the wealth-building process, *Worry-Free Family Finances* will empower you and your family to gain a strategic personal

6

financial advantage. The next 10 to 20 years will see the biggest wealth transfer in the history of humankind (from our parents to their children and grandchildren), estimated at $14 trillion in this country alone. The people inheriting all this money (which is almost all of us) need to know what to do with it, especially women, who (1) traditionally are paid less than men and tend to be in and out of the workforce for child rearing and caring for their elders, (2) will outlive men by 8 to 10 years, (3) will inherit money from their husbands and life partners, and (4) may know even less about money than men do.

Every person is different. Every family is different. Everyone has a different perspective and background. Everyone has a different degree of financial knowledge. Thus, there is no one-size-fits-all strategy that works for every individual and family every time. However, just as in being healthy, advancing your career, running a better household, and being a helpful volunteer, there are certain guidelines that always apply from the start.

If you feel you've started poorly or basically haven't started at all, *Worry-Free Family Finances* is for you. We liken managing your finances to the Kentucky Derby, the most famous horse race in the world and the world's oldest major sporting event. To win the race, first the horse has to get to the track. Second, it has to get into the starting gate. Third, it has to be pointed in the right direction. Fourth, it has to move forward when the gate opens. If the horse doesn't do even any one of these things, it has no chance to win. If it does them all, it has a fine shot because all it has to do is follow the track in the right direction.

That's the way we feel about this book. The useful and practical information in these pages is easily digestible, some of it even for younger children, and no previous knowledge is required, only the good common sense we know you already possess. The basics you need to know are contained within it. They are your blueprints to worry-free financial prosperity.

> *It isn't how much money a person makes in his life;*
> *it's how one manages one's income and finds peace.*
> —Author unknown

THE SEVEN-POINT CHECKLIST OF WORRY-FREE ATTITUDES FOR FINANCIAL SUCCESS

You may not like tests—we think few people do—but this is a fun one we made up that's easy to complete. Oh, go ahead. Take it. Nobody will know how you did but you. Quickly answer yes or no to each question and finish in less than a minute. We encourage all family members willing to take the test to do so.

1. I am objective about what money can and cannot do for me. I know exactly how I feel about money: attitudes, values, and comfort level.
2. I am competent to manage and control my money. (Of course you are. Give yourself a yes on this one.)
3. Managing money is a family affair.
4. I am involved in all financial decisions.
5. I make financial decisions as they come and don't put them off.
6. I don't treat money too seriously.
7. My plan for managing my money is simple and hassle-free.

If you answered yes to all seven statements, you're fiscally fit. You almost certainly are doing an excellent job with your money. Our job is to help you do it even better. Five to six trues show that you're getting strong. You're striving to get a perfect seven.

Three to four trues mean you're in basic training, financial boot camp if you will, while one or two trues indicate problems for sure. You're either a total wreck or nearly a total wreck. That's the bad news. But you're not hopeless because you've started turning your financial life around by buying this book. That's the good news.

You can get where you need to get financially just as well as anyone else can, with our help every step of the way. Fortunately for you and your family, working a lot longer and harder at your current occupation (aren't you already working longer and harder than you want to?) is not the only way to do that.

WHY YOU'RE WORRIED ABOUT MONEY

We were inspired to write this book because of our admiration for Henry David Thoreau, best known for his book *Walden* written in 1854.

Thoreau was an American writer, philosopher, and naturalist who lived for two years beside Walden Pond on the outskirts of Concord, Massachusetts, where "the shot heard round the world" helped end the Revolutionary War.

He went there to contemplate, study nature, meditate, read, and immerse himself in long conversations with friends. All that was an attempt to simplify his life, which he believed had become far too complicated.

We heartily agree with Thoreau's advice to "simplify, simplify" in all aspects of life, especially when it comes to money. Most individuals and families lead far too complicated financial lives, and we certainly have been guilty of that ourselves. Simplicity is more than just an ultimate destination. It's a continuous journey.

Financial simplicity is what this book is all about: powerful ways to make managing your and your family's money easier and more profitable so that money is no longer a problem, a worry, or a bother. The simple organized steps we outline will help make your financial affairs not only more rewarding but also much less complex and time-consuming, plus you'll have fun using our techniques.

Having advised more than 100,000 individuals about their personal finances through our newsletters, books, albums, seminars, personal coaching sessions, and hands-on money management, we know how

A bank is a place where they lend you an umbrella in fair weather and ask for it back when it begins to rain.

ROBERT FROST

worried and frustrated people are about money. We have been there too, and so has almost every other American. Yet America is the most prosperous nation in history. Economically, times are excellent even though the economy sometimes softens or even enters a recession. So what's the problem? We think lagging incomes are the principal culprit.

What do we mean? Let's suppose you are 45, are married, and have two children who will be learning from this book with you. Your household income (based on U.S. Commerce Department statistics) is $40,000, but that's before taxes. After taxes it's $32,000. Worse, that $32,000 is only $3000 more than it was 20 years ago, which means your after-tax household income hasn't kept up with inflation. Increases in the annual cost of living have grown about twice as fast as your spendable income, putting more and more American families like yours into potential financial jeopardy. Fortunately, there is a way out of this dilemma, and that's what *Worry-Free Family Finances* will help you do: escape financial distress.

The average American lives from paycheck to paycheck. According to the Department of Commerce, American households could survive roughly 90 days if both spouses lost their jobs. Credit-card debt alone works out to about $8400 per adult and is rising. It's a paradox that while "the great American money-making machine" remains alive and well, many citizens are faring poorly when it comes to their money.

While incomes have lagged, the financial arena has become more complex—and is covered more in the media—than ever. Television, radio, and the Internet are focused on the hour-to-hour, day-to-day fluctuations of the stock market and the economy. Daily, weekly, and monthly the financial presses churn out millions of words about stocks, bonds, mutual funds, leveraged buyouts, initial public offerings, and the like.

Best-seller lists over the years have been and still are crammed with books about doing this or that with your money. For the most part, those books are written by men and women who are excellent writers but who are not—let us repeat, not—financial experts and money managers.

These people sometimes write about money and personal finances as if these were something only a limited few can understand. But anyone can learn how to handle money wisely. Even preteens and teenagers can be successful investors. In fact, they are more trainable than adults.

Why? Because unlike most adults, they don't fret about the economy, what the Federal Reserve is doing or going to do, whether interest rates are rising or falling, whether the economy is in recession, and who's in charge of the White House. The list goes on and on of all the things they don't get concerned or upset about or even know about. What most young people want to do, once they understand the basics of investing, is one simple thing: accumulate shares of companies they know and trust. They want to get as many more of those shares as quickly and as often as they can. Period!

A few years ago we were called by a radio talk-show host about speaking on his program. However, the host expressed doubts about our claim to be able to show anyone how to become a multimillionaire on as little as $50 a month. After a few minutes' discussion he still wasn't a believer, so we asked, "What do we need to do to convince you that our method really works?" He responded, "Send your materials to my 12-year-old son, Brandon. If he likes what you send and understands it on his own, I'll have you on my show."

Three months later we were on the show with the host and Brandon. Both the father and the son asked several excellent questions about personal finances and investing. Then we asked Brandon, "Do you have a job?" He explained that he ran a newspaper route and earned $160 a month. He was putting half the money—$80 a month—to work as we had taught him to do and using the rest for things he wanted to buy. When his dad said, "Son, is this really as simple as the Statons claim it is?" Brandon shot back, "Dad, this is so simple, even you can do it." You and your family can do it too.

STATONS' IRON LAW: SAVINGS = INVESTMENT

We believe in Statons' iron law: Savings = Investment. There's no way to invest money for you and your family's future if you haven't saved any. Before you learn to invest wisely, you must learn to save more. The easiest way to start saving more is to eliminate at least some of, if not most of, all the wasteful spending habits we all have. We'll teach you how to improve in all key areas.

Our aim is to prepare you to make the major financial decisions that more and more Americans are being required to make but may not be prepared for, such as self-directing the investments in your retirement accounts, deciding how to manage an inheritance or a cash settlement from a divorce, getting your children through college without breaking your back or your bank account, and providing for your own long-term health care.

We know how well our advice works for young people. For 18 years Bill has been teaching Junior Achievement students in our hometown how to invest small amounts of money by using the guidelines in this book. These high schoolers not only learn how to invest their money, they actually do it, each using about $300 to $400 on average of their own money to get started.

Early in 2000 Bill was stopped by one of his former students at a local McDonald's. The young man took Bill's investing class when he was a junior in high school, started with about $350, and was adding $50 per month to his portfolio like clockwork while in college two years later. He is very typical, and best of all, he's made money.

We'll also share the story of our friend Willie Mae McDonald and her grandson Tremaine Tyson, fondly known as Tre.

When Tre graduated from high school in 1994, Bill invited him to lunch and suggested that he begin the "invest wisely" program outlined in this book. After an hour or so Bill said, "Read the information I'm giving you, and when you're ready to get started, call me. I'll help you."

Bill and Mary saw Tre about six months later and asked him when he wanted to start investing. Tre responded, "I already did. Your material is so easy to understand, I did it on my own."

Tre went to college on a scholarship in North Carolina, double-majored, and graduated with honors. At school he taught many of his friends the Staton method of investing. Some started their own investment programs, beginning with small amounts of money just as Tre had. When Tre graduated from college, he told us he'd invested roughly $3000 over eight semesters. In just four years his money had more than doubled. Tre's investment program gave him a great financial start. At age 22 he was well ahead of most of his peers and a lot of adults as well.

Regardless of the amount of money you have, it's easy and inexpensive to get started. These young people are the proof.

Before we go further, let's make sure you understand the true meaning of *investing*, a word so widely misunderstood that it frequently strikes fear in the hearts of a lot of people. Investing is not a great sacrifice or risk as most people think. Rather, *invest* comes from the Latin *investire*, which means "to clothe, to cover."

At a formal religious service the minister or priest will be attired "in" a "vestment," which is the origin of the word *investment*. Investing helps us all take care of basic needs such as clothing and shelter and when done wisely also allows us to enjoy many of the extra nice things in life.

An early but awkward definition of investing was "to set aside with thought of future benefit." Today we know it as putting money where it will earn a return: interest-bearing checking and savings accounts, your own business, real estate, bonds, stocks, mutual funds, and a host of highly specialized areas that include antiques, old coins, and art.

You most likely have money in a bank where it draws interest. If that is the case, you are already an investor even though you may never have thought of yourself as one. Having some money in the bank is fine, but you won't get wealthy that way. We show you later why owning a piece (shares) of the bank is a far better alternative. Willie Sutton supposedly said he robbed banks because "that's where the money is." Willy was wrong. Owning shares of a profitable bank or any other moneymaking enterprise is really where the money is.

Building wealth is not a great secret as the financial community might lead you to believe. They would like you to think that managing your own money is so tedious and treacherous, not to mention time-consuming, that it's best left to the "experts." Being in charge of your money doesn't have to be complicated once you know what to do and what not to do.

Managing your money should be simple, requiring only a few hours a year, as well as exciting and fun. It is exciting because you'll be watching your money grow faster than you ever imagined. It is fun because you'll be in charge. Can you picture how much self-confidence and satisfaction that will bring, not to mention the financial rewards? We've found that children often get a lot more excited than their parents do.

Wealth is largely a result of habit.
—John Jacob Astor

MEET SOME SUCCESS STORIES

Let us introduce you to one lady who proved that wealth is largely a result of habit. Imagine never earning more than $9000 in any year yet giving away more than $2 million. That's exactly what Florence Gray in Cleveland accomplished. Before her death at age 89 in 1993, she built a fortune in excess of $2.5 million and left almost all of it to two nursing schools.

Her starting salary as a market researcher for a midwestern newspaper, the *Plain Dealer*, was $19.27 a week in 1924. When she retired 45 years later as a market research supervisor, Florence Gray's annual salary was only $8996, $173 per week before taxes.

Described as an "absolute stickler for detail" and a "number cruncher" long before computers were widely available, Gray applied many of the key principles you'll learn in our book, including how to invest wisely, eliminate waste, and save more so that your money works as hard for you as you work to get it.

Although we never worked with Ms. Gray, in 1996 we had the pleasure of coaching a couple who were very much Ms. Gray's opposite. Bill and Diane are both Lutheran ministers, the nicest, most genuine people you'd ever want to meet. They were also clueless about money.

Two years after working with Bill and Diane, we received the following unsolicited letter from them. With their permission we've included part of it here because it proves not only that our wealth-building principles work but also that building wealth and getting yourself financially squared away don't require a Ph.D. in finance. Also, as you'll see from their letter, making money can be both easy and fun.

"My wife Diane and I began this journey after feeling a nagging lack of information as to how to properly budget, how to invest safely without being too conservative, and how to plan for the retirement years (a concern for me since I did not begin participating in any pension plan until I was 40).

"We used to dread sitting down together to discuss our finances. With no budget, no plan, no idea as to what we would need at retirement, no information or helpful models within our circles, we were discouraged about our financial future. If something were ever to happen to me, all I would have to leave for Diane was a term life insurance policy. I wanted to do better for her sake.

"Then . . . I found the Statons' book *The America's Finest Companies Investment Plan*, thanks to an article. [That book is now out of print.] After reading it (I couldn't put it down), I read it again. Bill's honesty, integrity, warmth and passion for helping people struck a responsive chord within me. 'We can surely trust this guy,' I thought. My family and I sold a small parcel of land and Diane and I used the remainder after taxes to enter the stock market (a first for both of us). That's where our journey began.

"1. We Now Have a Plan: Together Diane and I chose 10 companies from the Statons' AFC universe [you'll learn more about that list in the "Invest Wisely" chapter]. This was so much fun and gave us such enthusiasm and hope for what this initial investment could be in 25 years that we decided that we should clean up our finances, eliminate waste, pay down debt, save and set aside more money for investing. We estimate the Statons saved us $90,000 with two wealth-building ideas alone.

"2. Remarkable Portfolio Performance. After one year our portfolio gained 39.6 percent. To date, it has gained 44 percent along with stock splits, which have accrued more shares in some of our companies.

"3. Simple but Profound Paradigm Shifts: The more we save, the more we desire to invest. The more we invest, the more the portfolio grows. The more the portfolio grows, the more excited we get. The more excited we get, the more money we find to invest. The whole cycle begins again.

"4. An Old Dream with a New Vision: This leads me to share another important shift. We have noticed ourselves become investors, not just consumers. Investing is a way of life, a spiritual core value. Because we have stood on the shoulders of Bill and Mary Staton, we have seen farther than we could see for ourselves in the world of investing. We asked God to seriously help us do better with our finances. Now you know how he chose to answer our prayers." [The Reverends Bill and Diane have since adopted three babies and are putting each of them on a sound financial path.]

Like Bill and Diane, you can achieve all the financial security and independence you and your family desire. We wish you all the finest that life and money have to offer. Here's to all the success you can create!

Smart

My dad gave me one dollar bill
'Cause I'm his smartest son,
And I swapped it for two shiny quarters
'Cause two is more than one.
And then I took the quarters
And traded them to Lou
For three dimes—I guess he don't know
That three is more than two.
Just then, along came old blind Bates
And just 'cause he can't see
He gave me four nickels for my three dimes,
And four is more than three.
And I took the nickels to Hiram Coombs
Down at the seed-feed store,
And the fool gave me five pennies for them,
And five is more than four.
And then I went and showed my dad,
And he got red in the cheeks
And closed his eyes and shook his head—
Too proud of me to speak.

—Shel Silverstein

2

Dream Often and Dream Big

What you think upon grows.
— *ORIENTAL MAXIM*

What you think you become.
— *GAUTAMA BUDDHA*

As you think, so shall you become.
— *JESUS OF NAZARETH*

Bill's religion professor in college, Dr. Bernard Boyd, was one of the most colorful people Bill had ever known. He told many wonderful stories that brought the Old Testament to life in a way his students never would have believed possible. One of his best stories was about Albert Einstein.

While young Bernard was a seminary student at Princeton, Einstein was a professor well known for his absentminded ways. On more than one occasion Boyd saw the famous theoretician and scientist wandering aimlessly in the middle of the street licking an ice cream cone, totally oblivious to traffic and the potential threat to his life.

One day Bernard Boyd, late for a class, was rushing down the library steps and accidentally bumped into Dr. Einstein, almost knocking the two of them down. Stunned, he realized who it was and hurriedly apologized. Einstein was polite and said he should not worry about it.

What happened next was a complete surprise. Boyd, who was almost speechless, blathered, "Why don't you come to my room tonight around eight and meet some of my friends." Einstein said that sounded like fun, so he'd be there.

The rest of the day Boyd told all his friends to come by his room that evening because Big Al was going to be there. When they asked, "Who's Big Al?" the response was, "It'll be fun. Just come." So they did. A small crowd gathered in anticipation of meeting Big Al, who as almost always was late.

Around 8:20 a few people were starting to leave when suddenly Albert Einstein appeared and asked for Bernard Boyd. At first some of the friends thought the man was an impostor, even a hired prankster, but they soon realized it really was Albert Einstein in the flesh.

Dr. Boyd related that Albert Einstein was very friendly, answered lots of questions, and participated in a "bull session" typical of any-one's college days. Einstein was said to be "colorful" and "lively," and that leads us to another story about him and big dreams, the subject of this chapter.

Einstein has always been regarded as one of the greatest minds on the planet if not the greatest of all time. Scientists had a special desire to study his brain, and he granted their wish under one condition that would take place after his death. He handed the scientists a sealed enve-lope with specific instructions that they be read only after the scientists finished their research, which, strangely enough, took place at Cornell University rather than Princeton.

Einstein died a few years later. After weeks of intensive study of his brain and much debate among the scientists, they called a press confer-ence to discuss their findings. Yes, they'd uncovered a major difference between Einstein's brain and everyone else's. No, it wasn't the differ-ence everyone had expected. Einstein's brain was about three-quarters the size of a normal human adult's. Other than that there was no dis-cernible difference.

After that stunning press announcement, the sealed envelope was opened, and its one-sentence contents read: "I do not consider myself to be especially smarter than any other human, but I do have a particu-larly vivid imagination."

Our only limits are in our imagination.
—Albert Einstein

It was Einstein's vivid imagination, his ability to dream and dream big, that gave the world the incredible theory of relativity and the equally incredible equation $e = mc^2$ (energy = mass times the speed of light squared).

Einstein's active use of his imagination, his strong ability to see things as they could be in his dreams, was what really separated him from so many other scientists. Einstein was one of the most famous dreamers of all time, and we use him as a premier example of someone who could make his wildest dreams come true. He must have been the model for W. Clement Stone's famous saying, "What the mind can conceive can be achieved."

YOU CAN CONCEIVE AND ACHIEVE WHATEVER YOU WANT

Clement Stone, a short man with a pencil-thin mustache who donned colorful vests and vibrant suspenders, passed away in September 2002 at the age of 100. The *New York Times* noted that he "parlayed" $100 in savings into an insurance empire. Clement Stone was a firm believer in the power of positive thinking and turning dreams into reality. He was a huge giver as well and is known to have dispensed nearly $300 million to charities ranging from mental health to youth-welfare groups. Stone said, "All I want to do is change the world," and based on his life, he did, in a most positive way. No doubt dozens of millions more will be given to worthwhile causes as Stone's estate is settled.

William Clement Stone was a big dreamer despite the fact that his father died when he was only three, impoverished by heavy gambling losses. He sold newspapers in Chicago at age 6, owned his own newsstand by age 13, and started working with his mother in her little insurance agency when he was 16, all the while soaking up Horatio Alger stories of poor boys making good.

Until one is committed, there is hesitancy, the chance to draw back,
always ineffectiveness. Concerning acts of initiative and creation,

there is one elementary truth the ignorance of
which kills countless ideas and splendid plans:
that the moment one definitely commits oneself,
then Providence moves too.
All sorts of things occur to help one that would
never otherwise have occurred.
A whole stream of events issues from the decision,
raising in one's favor all manner of unforeseen incidents
and meetings and material assistance,
which no one could have dreamt would come their way.
Whatever you can do, or dream you can, begin it.
Boldness has genius, power, and magic in it. Begin it now.

—Goethe

Stone managed to build the small insurance business into an empire, and in the middle of the Depression in 1930 he employed more than 1000 agents as representatives of large casualty companies. His Combined Insurance Company of America changed names and became Aon Corp. in 1987. In early 2001 the company begin paying a higher annual cash dividend to its shareowners for the fifty-second consecutive year, one of the finest performances of any public company in the world.

Clement Stone was a shrewd businessman who dreamed huge dreams and believed that nothing was impossible for him to achieve as long as he kept those things in the forefront of his mind. The same is true for you and your family, particularly if your dream is to make your and your family's finances worry-free. Keeping your money dreams in the forefront of your mind will enable you to create a worry-free family financial lifestyle.

In building his insurance empire Stone liked to use other people's money to acquire additional insurance companies. For example, he borrowed money from the Commercial Credit Company to purchase Pennsylvania Casualty Company, which in fact was owned by none other than Commercial Credit. Stone became famous for espousing PMA (positive mental attitude), and it must have worked in spades in all his personal and business endeavors.

My dream was to see my name on the cover of a book.
If you've got dreams, follow them.
Even if they don't make you rich, they make you happy.
—Tom Clancy

Reverend Dr. Robert Schuller started a church near Pasadena, California, in 1955 in a drive-in movie theater with only a few dozen weekly attendees, many of them curious to see what type of person would undertake such a thing. Today his weekly Sunday program *Hour of Power* is broadcast across the globe, reaching hundreds of millions of people. Dr. Schuller said he was born during a flood "at the dead end of a dirt road that had no name and no number" and noted that from the time he was five years old his "dream" was to become a preacher.

At Western Theological Seminary he learned that when you have a burning desire along with a dream, "you can go anywhere from nowhere." He has long fought the battle to eliminate the word *impossible* from human thinking. His life and success prove he's on the right track. If you read even quickly through his book *My Journey*, you will find the word *dream* over and over. The man who coined the phrase "Possibility Thinking" is definitely one who believes that no dream is impossible—no, not even one. And he lives that dream philosophy as well. Dr. Schuller knows, "If you can dream it, you can do it."

Our friend Don Clair says that adults need to "give kids the tools that make them dream." Don devised a revolutionary program, for which he has been recognized nationally, to help prison inmates return to the "real world" prepared to meet the challenges of life, especially the financial ones. We first met Don through Anthony Robbins, "Mr. Personal Power," who asked if Bill might go to St. Louis and show the inmates at a nearby federal prison how to manage their money wisely.

Not only did Bill work with the inmates at the federal correctional institute, he also "coached" the warden and his staff as well as the spouses of a group of male prisoners. In addition, Bill worked with a group of disadvantaged high school students through Don to teach them that financial dreams—coming out of almost any circumstance—

can be achieved if we only believe them. Don's dream to help others became a positive experience for hundreds of inmates and for the classes of young people he worked with to give them tools to make their dreams a reality.

Most people will never be a household name and face as was Rex David Thomas, widely known as the founder of Wendy's, who passed away in 2002 at age 69, having starred in more than 800 television commercials. Thomas was an orphan who started working in restaurants at age 12 and ended up heading the third largest hamburger chain in the world. Dave Thomas became a world champion at promoting the adoption of foster children because he was adopted and knew their need for love.

A fan of the *Popeye* cartoon series, Thomas said that Wimpy was his favorite character because he loved hamburgers. The famous Wendy's square burger was the product of advice from his grandmother, who instilled in young David the idea that he should "never cut corners." Failing to finish high school by age 18, Dave Thomas later hired a tutor in 1993 to help him pass the G.E.D. examination. Fort Lauderdale high school in Coconut Creek honored him as part of its senior class at graduation, and Thomas and his wife of 47 years, Lorraine, were named king and queen of their prom. Not surprisingly, Thomas was dubbed "most likely to succeed."

Most of us grow up hearing about setting goals, but rarely do any of us talk about dreaming dreams. There is a vast difference between the two. Goals are necessary and great, but dreams are much greater. Let us explain.

Even when he was a young boy, Bill's parents and grandparents (especially his grandfather, John Staton) taught him to set goals, to set his sights on the targets he wanted to hit. Bill remembers entering the Pitt County science fair in the eighth grade after having set the goal of winning first prize for his solar energy project, and he won the blue ribbon.

Throughout high school Bill set a variety of goals: to make the Beta Club, to win first prize in a magazine sales contest, to be valedictorian of his senior class (that wasn't too tough; there were only 22 graduates), to work every summer, to go to camp, and to become an Eagle and God and Country Boy Scout, to name just a few and to let you know what he did achieve!

Other goals were to graduate from the University of North Carolina at Chapel Hill (Michael Jordan graduated from there a few years later) and to earn an MBA in finance from a top business school, the University of Pennsylvania's Wharton School, rated today as it was then the number one graduate school of business in the world.

Still another goal was to become either a security analyst or a money manager and live no farther north than Richmond, Virginia, or farther west than the Mississippi River. Bill ended up in Charlotte, North Carolina, in 1971 with a regional brokerage firm, Interstate Securities, which is now part of Wachovia Corp. He achieved all the principal goals there he originally set out to achieve, including becoming head of the equity research department, a member of the management team, and a director of the firm.

It was only when Bill struck out on his own in late 1985 to write a monthly financial newsletter that he discovered the enormous difference between goals and dreams and why the latter are so much more powerful than the former. Once he had that realization, Bill began to teach achieving all of one's financial dreams in his (now our) wealth-building seminars. Many attendees say it's one of the finest, most useful skills they've learned and wonder why they haven't seen it elsewhere. Now we get to share it with you, which is one of our biggest dreams.

A *goal* is defined as "an objective; the finish line of a race." In Merrie Olde England, it was a "boundary." If we asked you to list some of the positive and negative attributes of a goal, what would you say? One obvious positive is that a goal gives you something to shoot at, to reach, a target. There's nothing wrong with that, especially if you set goals that make you stretch to achieve them.

Jack Welch, former masterful chief executive officer (CEO) of General Electric, set "stretch" goals for GE each year. Although the company never seemed to reach goals such as a certain amount of inventory turnover and a particular level of operating margin, he and the management team raised them for the next year anyway. They believed, and we firmly agree, that stretching for a goal and not reaching it is better than meeting a goal that's easy to attain. General Electric has amassed the impressive corporate numbers to prove it.

Another positive is that goals give us something to measure against. For example, we want to sell 100,000 subscriptions to our newsletter each year, and we're not there yet. As we move toward the 100,000 target, we can chart our progress to see how well we're doing and whether we're going backward or forward.

A third positive is that a goal is tangible. As a fellow named Gil Atkinson said, "The clearer and more vividly you visualize a goal, the easier it becomes to achieve or acquire it. Ride in it, fly in it, get pictures of it. Then list the steps to attain it."

Please don't get us wrong. We are not against goals. What we don't like is that when you set any goal, it automatically becomes a limit. Limits may hinder progress. We have no other objections to goals except that it's easy to set a goal that's no challenge to meet.

GOALS VERSUS DREAMS

Let's say you and your family are making $40,000 a year and want to double that within five years to $80,000. The $80,000 automatically becomes a cap because that's your goal. Once you get to $80,000 you're capped out because you have reached your target. You say to us, "But Mary and Bill, once I reach one goal, all I need to do is make another one that's even bolder than the one before." We say, "Of course you can do that, but there's a much better path." Dream and dream *big*.

Contrast the definition of a goal with that of a dream: "a wild fancy or hope; a condition that is longed for; having a deep aspiration." *Dream* comes from the Middle English word *drem* ("joy, music") and the Old Saxon word *drom* ("mirth"). There is truly so much joy, music, and mirth in every dream.

We exhort you to dream often and dream *big*. A dream, unlike a goal, has no boundaries. It's boundaryless. Everything is possible in a dream. There are no limits.

Few people anywhere in the world recognize the name Don Clayton, a fellow Tarheel, from Fayetteville, North Carolina. But he founded a business most of us instantly recognize—Putt-Putt—and built the first course in his hometown in 1954. Miniature golf everywhere is known as Putt-Putt just as tissues are universally recognized as Kleenex.

Before he passed away from a heart attack at age 70, Clayton had built his company into a $100 million operation. Former Fayetteville Mayor J. L. Dawkins remembers that Don Clayton was a big dreamer. Clayton told him he was going to build courses all across North Carolina, then all across America, and then throughout the world, and he did. Dawkins said of Clayton, "Don dreamed dreams. He dreamed the dreams, and he followed through."

Don't just wish for a Ferrari. Dream of a fleet of Ferraris. Don't just have the goal of one nice home. How about multiple incredible homes at the beach, the mountains, the lake, in foreign countries? That's dreaming. Even if it seems impossible, dream it anyway if it's what you and your family really want. Goals can hold you back. Dreams never do. Dreams are limitless, and there's never an end to the number of dreams you can dream.

Woodrow Wilson, the twenty-eighth president of the United States, said, "We grow great by dreams." We know that to be true because dreaming works for us. Since learning the Silva method of making mind pictures some years ago, we've spent a lot more time picturing and dreaming and writing down on paper the things we want for ourselves, for our family, and for others. Bill does his most productive dreaming when he's relaxed and not doing anything else, such as when he is driving by himself on a long trip, when he's out in our woodsy backyard, or when he's on vacation.

Mary's most productive "dream moments" are her quiet time in meditation or when she is actively "dreaming" while wide awake and writing down those dreams. Mary began doing this in her first professional job fresh out of college. She wrote down five dreams she wanted to come true by the time she reached age 30 and placed the list in the bottom drawer of her dresser. Mary found her list a few weeks before her thirtieth birthday and discovered that all five dreams had come true, including having her first baby by that age.

The more relaxed you are, the more dreams you'll have, along with the specific directions on how to reach them.

We keep a dream list in our computer to which we continually add. It's sectioned into a variety of categories and is growing longer and longer. It seems that the longer that list gets, the faster our dreams come true. In addition we've noticed that compared to the way it was before we started actively dreaming, a lot of worthwhile dreams we hadn't even thought about or put down on paper have come true too. It surely is exciting when they do.

Our friend Mark Victor Hansen, coauthor of the best-selling *Chicken Soup for the Soul* series, and Bill interviewed each other on a two-hour audiocassette in early 1997. Mark pointed out that he had put more than 6000 dreams in writing and more than 1500 had come true. If that's not proof that dreaming is powerful, we don't know what is.

By the way, Mark and his coauthor Jack Canfield have the mental and written dream to sell—are you ready for this?—500 million *Chicken Soup* books. We won't be surprised when they do it because dreaming and dreaming big make big things come true. It works for Mark and Jack. It works for us. It will work for you too.

> *If you will make the decision,*
> *your subconscious will make the provision.*
> —Author unknown

Earl Nightingale, founder of Nightingale-Conant and one of the country's greatest motivational speakers and writers, produced the hugest-selling single audiocassette in history, *The Strangest Secret*. Decades later it is still immensely popular and continues selling well year after year.

Earl Nightingale was a tremendous inspiration to us and millions of others who said and wrote many useful things we've taken to heart. When he wrote the following five sentences, he was talking about goals. Everywhere the word *goal* was used we've substituted the word *dream*, which we think makes Nightingale's words that much stronger. We believe he would approve the change:

> *A dream gives the picture to the subconscious.*
> *Dreams motivate us. They give us things to look forward to.*
> *Dreams give us drive and energy to stay on the success track.*
> *Our dreams work for us while we sleep.*

Let's analyze just what Nightingale said, line by line. "A dream gives the picture to the subconscious." The subconscious (an even better name is the superconscious because this part of the brain is super) is the highest part of the mind, the part that is always at work, that always knows what is best for us and is never distracted by the incessant chatter of the conscious mind. A dream is a big picture, a giant photograph impressed on the superconscious mind. That superconscious mind then begins to work on making it come true. You can afford to dream gigantic, as gigantic as you want, no matter how abstractly, because the details of reaching a dream will come. They always do.

"Dreams motivate us. They give us things to look forward to." In *Built to Last*, James C. Collins and Jerry I. Porras say that Sam Walton, the founder of Wal-Mart Stores, went into business with a strong desire to work for himself and a "lot of passion" about retailing. In an interview with The *New York Times* Walton recounted, "I had no vision of the scope of what I would start, but I always had confidence that as long as we did our work well and were good to our customers, there would be no limit to us."

Note what Walton said: "No limit." Talk about a gigantic dream. Sam Walton began the most successful retailing enterprise in the world with one five-and-dime-store franchise in 1945. The reason? His dream was that there was no cap on how big a company he could grow. Wal-Mart Stores is now the largest employer outside of government anywhere in the world.

"Dreams give us drive and energy to stay on the success track." Charlie Young, a man from our hometown of Charlotte whom we've met only once, bought a remote piece of land off the coast of North Carolina near Wilmington in 1972. He named it Middle Island and paid nearly $500,000 to acquire it from a company that was on the verge of bankruptcy. Why did he buy it? Charlie said that as far back as he could remember he'd always dreamed of buying an island. So when the chance came to do it, he pounced, knowing full well he could easily lose his entire investment. There were so many unknowns at the time of the purchase and things to be done to make it work. But Charlie never let up and has made millions, all from one dream he had in childhood. He never gave up trying to make his big dream come true.

"Our dreams work for us while we sleep." Wolfgang Amadeus Mozart, one of the foremost composers of all time, used to dream an entire piece of music, wake up the next morning, and put it all down on paper. It is said that he rarely edited any of his musical scores because they were perfected in his superconscious mind as he slept and dreamed.

Shortly after Bill and Mary met in 1990, she wrote down six big dreams for Bill and her children on a slip of paper and filed it away in a drawer. When we married in 1994 and were moving Mary's family's things into our new home, she found them and showed them to Bill.

Four had already come true, including having a book, *The America's Finest Companies® Investment Plan*, published by a national firm in 1994 (now out of print). A fifth dream was about to come true, and we both felt strongly that the sixth would as well. It did.

In our seminars across the country we talk about the almost unbelievable power of dreams and give out the simple handout below for our audience members to fill in. They usually take about five to seven minutes.

On the first five lines we ask them, as we're asking you now (please have each family member do this separately), to list the top five most important financial dreams they'd like to reach within the next five years. On the next three lines we ask them to list three 90-day financial dreams. Most important, we tell them that they don't have to be too specific and to think huge, not small. The sky is literally the limit, even if they don't believe it.

At this point we're reminded of the wonderful letter we received from seven-year-old Michael Hutchison of La Jolla, California, after he'd read our guidebook (with the help of his dad) called *How to Become a MultiMillionaire on Just $50 a Month* (which has been incorporated into this book) and begun implementing its strategy to convert small amounts of money into a large fortune.

Young Mike said he was going to maintain the program for a long, long time and contribute money to it each month, and he emphasized that he would be worth $5 million by the time he was 12. Kids are naturally big dreamers. It's a shame so many adults aren't. Mike is one big dreamer who'll end up with all the money he'll ever need while he's still young enough to enjoy it.

It's your turn to make your and your family's dreams come true. We've painted the big picture about dreams. Now's the time to put it to the test. Go ahead. Write down your biggest long-term and near-term financial dreams. We'll wait. Dream your impossible dreams!

The simple act of writing down a dream and making a plan for its accomplishment moves you to the top 3 percent.
—Brian Tracy

The World's Most Powerful WealthBuilding Technique®

Write your and your family's top five money dreams for the next five years:

1.

2.

3.

4.

5.

Next write your and your family's top three money dreams for the next 90 days:

1.

2.

3.

We don't know who said this, but the author was on the money: "Write it down. This is the way to transform wishes into wants; can'ts into cans; dreams into plans; and plans into reality. Don't just think it—ink it."

Congratulations! You've just done something most people unfortunately will never do unless we get to them through this book or, even better, unless you share this simple, powerful technique with everyone you know. It works just as well in business life as it does in personal and family life. In fact, we can't think of any place it doesn't work.

We are grateful that Nightingale-Conant produced an album by Bill called *The Seven Secrets to Becoming a Multimillionaire.* Earl Nightingale and Victor Conant founded the company many years ago in Chicago, and it is now run by Conant's son, Vic. He produces a free weekly *Achievement Newsletter: The Inspiration You Need to Succeed,* which we would encourage you to get because it will help you in pursuing all your dreams (go to www.nightingale.com to sign up; there is absolutely no obligation). Once you sign up, Vic encourages you to "forward this newsletter to anyone who you feel could benefit from these powerful messages," so Nightingale-Conant is living "give more," one of the three cornerstones of *Worry-Free Family Finances.*

Nightingale said decades ago, "It is understanding emotionally as well as intellectually that we literally become what we think about, that we must control our thoughts if we're to control our lives. It's understanding fully that 'as ye sow, so shall ye reap.'

"It's cutting away all fetters from the mind and permitting it to soar as it was divinely designed to do. It's the realization that your limitations are self-imposed and that the opportunities for you today are enormous beyond belief.

"It's using all your courage to force yourself to think positively . . . to let your imagination speculate freely. And to keep constantly aware of the fact that you are, at this moment, standing in the middle of your own 'acres of diamonds.'

"Finally, take action—ideas are worthless unless we act on them."

You've written down eight money dreams you'd love to see come true. Do you believe they will? It's better than believing that they won't, but assuming that you're skeptical (at least at first), you've still unleashed a positive force no one can explain.

Are there really any limits to what can be dreamed and achieved, especially if you put your skills and your time and your money into serving others?

Remember George Washington Carver? He saw that what used to be called the goober pea (originally from Africa and now called the peanut) could do much more. Actually, he discovered more than 300 uses for the common peanut, including bleach, salve, paper, ink, rubber, linoleum, shampoo, wood filler, and pickle. Few people know he also uncovered more than 110 uses for another common crop, the sweet potato. How did he do that? He simply dreamed about it, over and over again.

Ever heard of Bill Porter? Johnson & Johnson, one of *America's Finest Companies*®, produced an excellent show called *Door to Door*, featuring cerebral palsy victim Bill Porter, in Portland, Oregon. Porter was born in San Francisco in 1932 with a twisted right side and slurred speech.

At his father's urging to get a job so that he wouldn't remain on disability, Bill Porter finally landed a sales position with Watkins Inc., this country's oldest door-to-door sales company.

Within the first year he began garnering sales awards and even crawled through part of his sales route (seven miles) one day during a blizzard. That turned out to be one of his finest sales days ever because most people were home.

Called "relentless" and "irresistible" by his boss, Porter would wake up before 5 a.m. to give himself a couple of hours to get dressed, then take a 7:30 bus to get to his territory by 9:00 a.m. His assistant still today and lifetime friend, Shelly Brady, says that when you meet Bill Porter and learn his story, you realize that what's important is really inside each of us. Porter, who is still living and working, shows us all that outward appearances do not matter.

Despite odds that would seem impossible to overcome, Bill Porter always had the dream that he would have a successful career. It never entered his mind "that I couldn't."

To Achieve Financial Dreams

1. They must be your and your family's.
2. They must be worthy.
3. They should be right for you and your family.
4. They must be in writing.
5. They will lead to a plan of action with specific steps and deadlines.
6. They will take time to achieve.
7. Begin only if you will continue.

Don't be afraid to dream,
for out of such fragile things come miracles.
—Author Unknown

THE PRESENT

Our son Will is a teenager. His friend at school shared this with him, and so Will brought it home, typed it into the computer, and sent it to close friends and family members. We were so taken with it, we decided to share it with you. It's entitled *The Present*, and we would love to know who authored it.

"Imagine there is a bank that credits your account each morning $86,400. It carries over no balance from day to day. Every evening the bank deletes whatever part of the balance you failed to use during the day. What would you do? Draw out every cent of course.

"Each of us has such a bank. Its name is TIME. Every morning, it credits you with 86,400 seconds. Every night this bank writes off, as lost, whatever of this you have failed to invest to good purpose. It carries over no balance. It allows no overdraft. Each day it opens a new account for you. Each night it burns the remains of the day. If you fail to use the day's deposits, the loss is yours.

"There is no going back. There is no drawing against tomorrow. You must live in the present on today's deposits. Invest it so as to get from it the utmost in health, happiness, and success. The clock is running. Make the most of today.

"To realize the value of ONE YEAR, ask a student who failed a grade.

"To realize the value of ONE MONTH, ask a mother who gave birth to a premature baby.

"To realize the value of ONE WEEK, ask the editor of a weekly newspaper.

"To realize the value of ONE HOUR, ask the lovers who are waiting to meet.

"To realize the value of ONE MINUTE, ask a person who missed the train.

"To realize the value of ONE SECOND, ask a person who just avoided a car accident.

"To realize the value of ONE MILLISECOND, ask the person who won a silver medal in the Olympics.

"Treasure every moment that you have. And if you shared it with someone special, treasure it more because you did share it with someone special, someone special enough to spend your time with. And remember that time waits for no one.

"Yesterday is history. Tomorrow is a mystery. Today is a gift. That's why it's called 'The Present.' "

Twenty years from now you will be more disappointed
by the things you didn't do
than by the ones you did do. So, throw off the bowlines.
Sail away from the safe harbor. Catch the trade winds in your sails.
Explore. Dream. Discover.

—H. Jackson Brown, Jr.

3

Save More

Get all you can, without hurting your soul,
your body or your neighbor.
Save all you can, cutting off every needless
expense.
Give all you can.

—JOHN WESLEY

A clergyman of the Church of England, John Wesley (1703–1791) was the founder of Methodism. Before that Wesley was a principal in what was then called an evangelical revival, in which the twin practices of having deep personal faith and performing good works were emphasized.

An itinerant preacher who traveled from parish to parish (an estimated 250,000 miles in his lifetime), John Wesley delivered more than 40,000 sermons, sometimes as many as four to five each day. Wesley's firm commitment to serving others, especially through the giving of money and talent, led to the quote above, which we believe sums up *Worry-Free Family Finances*. Let's break down exactly what the Reverend John Wesley said into three parts and show you how to put it into positive action.

1. "Get all you can, without hurting your soul, your body or your neighbor." Another way of expressing this would be that earning money, even a lot of it, through honest means is okay. Wesley advises specifically that you should earn your money "without hurting your soul [the inner part of you that discerns right from wrong], your body [stress is a major killer in U.S. society and in

many other industrialized nations as well] or your neighbor [we interpret that to mean other humans in general rather than only someone who lives next to you]."

2. "Save all you can, cutting off every needless expense." The wisdom of Benjamin Franklin comes in nicely here in the twin corollaries "waste not, want not" and "a penny saved is a penny earned." A needless expense is what we term wasted money, money that disappears very easily and is spent on things you really don't want or need. In short, stuff. Later on we'll get into how to reduce wasteful spending in more detail.

3. "Give all you can." Give all you can to help others whether it is a friend who's ill, working with Boy and Girl Scouts, or supporting the United Way. There are so many worthwhile places to give not only your money but also your time, your enthusiasm, and your ideas. In four words John Wesley simply said "give" and give "all you can."

Ours is a six-word, three-point wealth-building program to pull your family finances together and make them worry-free: Save more. Give more. Invest wisely. Another champion who lives these principles is Warren Buffett, the richest investor on the planet. We believe the "invest wisely" ideas we introduce in Chapter 5 are the closet thing to Buffett's philosophy on paper. For that reason alone they are worth knowing and applying to your and your own family's financial life.

Warren Buffett is an investing genius by anyone's standards, able to afford anything and everything he could ever want, yet he lives simply and unostentatiously. Unlike many millionaires and billionaires who live in glamorous locations such as New York, London, Beverly Hills, Monaco, and Hong Kong, Buffett resides in, of all places, Omaha, Nebraska. He's owned the same ranch-style home for most of his life and says that will be his residence when he dies. And he is a prolific saver who believes in not wasting shareowners' money.

The *New York Times* (July 23, 2000) described Buffett as a man who "plays the part of the hayseed . . . who loves bridge and jokes that he reluctantly drags himself around a golf course." A $10,000 stake in Warren Buffett's "holding-company-cum-investment-fund" in 1969 was worth about $39 million at the beginning of the new millennium. Buffett's company, Berkshire-Hathaway, according to the *Times*, "has minted many a millionaire and has made Mr. Buffett an American icon."

Almost anyone passing Warren Buffett on the street would not know who he is, and that's the way Buffett likes it. He is a bona fide investing celebrity who is almost unknown outside the financial world. In many ways Warren Buffett is a typical American in his early seventies and a man whose favorite foods are said to be Cherry Cokes and cheeseburgers. His favorite sport, as you might expect, is baseball. In fact, he owns a minor league baseball team, the Mudhens. In where else? Omaha.

Buffett treats money seriously but not too seriously and has a great sense of humor, particularly about himself. Like Hall of Fame catcher Yogi Berra, Buffett is widely quoted, and there are a number of well-written books about him (although Buffett says he will never pen one about himself).

One of our favorite and little-known "Buffettisms" is about the time he and his sister entered a shopping mall in Omaha. Upon spotting a phone, she said, "Warren, do you have money for a phone call?" Buffett's sister turned around and noticed he had disappeared. After several minutes Buffett returned, and she asked, "Where did you go?" He responded, "I went to get the correct change."

Can you picture a man worth billions of dollars spending five minutes to change two quarters for one 35-cent phone call? Warren Buffett lives and breathes the principle "Waste not, want not."

We hear all the time, "I don't have enough money to do what I want to do," but with a little bit of investigation we find that that usually isn't the case. We once met an employee of US Airways who said she'd always wanted to save and invest but never had the money. We suggested tracking her expenses to find "hidden" funds she didn't know were there.

Later in the conversation she confessed that she had eight cats and that they did not eat cat food: They dined on canned tuna, fresh fish, and other human delights. Did this lady have money to save and invest for her future? We say she did. But she was wasting it on human food for her cats.

Who can't cut back a little and not waste at least one or two dollars a day? That's $365 to $730 a year. Almost anyone can accumulate that much simply by dropping pocket change into a jar at the end of each day. One of our favorite companies, Clayton Homes in Nashville, Tennessee, is successful for many reasons, not the least of which is that the company believes in not wasting money.

In the early 1990s Clayton asked each of its employees, from the chief executive on down, to figure out multiple ways to save at least a dollar per person per day for an entire year. Employees were encouraged to share their ideas with others, submit them to top management, and have them published in the company newsletter. There were contests to see who could stop wasting the most money and to find the most creative ways to eliminate waste.

The campaign took hold and was far more successful than anyone ever imagined it would be. Hundreds of thousands of otherwise wasted dollars dropped straight to Clayton's bottom line. That boosted the stock price and enhanced the wealth of almost every Clayton employee because the overwhelming majority own shares.

We've found that everyone we've taught—students, professionals, retirees, the working homeless, inmates—wastes money. What do we mean by wasted money? It's money that just evaporates. It literally slips between your fingers (between the cracks), and you have no idea where it went. For people who budget it's usually the second largest figure behind the mortgage payment. Typically it's called "miscellaneous," aka "I don't know where all that money went, but it sure disappeared in a hurry."

How much money do you waste each day, each week, each month, each year? Our guess is it's between $200 and $400 a month ($2400 to $4800 a year) based on our experience and having personally surveyed hundreds of people of all ages from all walks of life.

Let us share with you what Bill's Junior Achievement students say. The first day of each class he talks about what economics really means and why it's important to every person. *Economics* comes from the Greek words *oikonomikos* or *oikonomos*, both of which refer to "managing your household."

They also can refer to "managing a state" and dealing with such things as bringing in revenue through taxation. The first recorded usage of our current word *economy* was discovered in a book about the construction of a monastery written around 1440.

Today *economics* and *economy* typically are thought to include the economic system of a state or nation, but certainly those terms are every bit as important when referring to managing your family's income and expenses in an organized manner. When we think of things like economy car, economy class, and being economical, that automatically takes us to thrift. Part of becoming comfortable if not very well off financially relates closely to being thrifty. Not cheap, thrifty. There is a *big* difference. Eliminating wasteful spending is one simple way to better manage your household and significantly reduce your and your family's worries about money.

After explaining why the art and science of managing the household better is important to everyone in a home, including Bill's students, he polls them one by one to see how much they estimate they waste. Almost without exception the answer is somewhere in the range of $15 to $30 a week, or $60 to $120 per month, and often more. We remember one kid sitting in the front row of one of Bill's classes. His answer to the question was $50. Bill remarked, "You mean you waste only $50 a month?" He shot back, "Oh, I thought you meant each week."

Bill asks each class of students to do the following exercise. You can use this simple and powerful technique to spot the waste, the leaks in your "financial ship" so to speak.

A SEVEN-DAY PLAN FOR REINING IN EXPENSES

For the next week, just seven days, carry around one or two four by six cards and something to write with. Outside ordinary bills such as electricity and groceries, we want you to write down every expense over $1.00 and what the money was spent for. It doesn't matter whether it's cash, a credit or debit card, or a check. Write it down. You'll quickly begin to see where a lot of your money is going and will easily discover some obvious leaks you were not aware of. Even the most conscientious savers are surprised by the amounts of money they waste.

At the end of the week (don't do it before then because it could get too scary and you might quit early), categorize the expenses as best you can: trips to the mall, teller machine withdrawals, and the like. Then add them all up. Now you've got a good handle on the money you're wasting, most likely without even knowing it, and you can take steps immediately to stop doing it. See the following chart for an example.

We've had some individuals call in to radio shows and tell us they live on such pathetic incomes that they don't have even a penny to waste. One was a nice elderly lady who claimed she could barely make ends meet even with Social Security as a supplement. She was adamant that she never wasted any money. "Never?" Mary asked. "Do you have grandchildren?" The lady said she did. Mary then asked, "Have you ever given them presents they stopped using after one or two days?" She replied, "Of course. That happens to everyone." Of course it does. That's one typical way parents and grandparents waste money. As a simple alternative, you could give them money to put into a bank savings account. Even better, you could help them invest wisely, as you'll learn to do in Chapter 5.

Retail malls are another wonderful place to waste money. They are so popular today that going to the mall is considered in certain circles to be a good way to exercise. Other people seem to think it's their patriotic duty to go at least once a week, if not more often. Still others, especially young people, go to hang out and see who else is hanging out.

Day 1 / Friday

Coffee / bran muffin	$ 4.00
ATM withdraw fee	3.00
Soft drink from machine	1.25
Snack from machine	.75
Lunch	6.95
Soft drink from machine	1.25
Chinese takeout for 4	32.00
Sweater on sale at mall	45.00
Blockbuster rental	4.00
Total	**$98.20**

When you go to malls, you're asking for trouble because you're setting yourself up to buy stuff you don't need even though that may not be your original intent. When you go to malls for nothing in particular, you will waste money. That's a guarantee, the only one in this book.

It's a beautiful Saturday morning (when you ought to be enjoying nature outside), and you get to your favorite mall around 11:30 a.m. Since you're short of cash (aren't we always?), you plop your ATM card into a machine and extract $20. Your friendly local bank charges you $1 to $3 (wasted money) for the "privilege" of getting your own money out. (Those bankers are smart, aren't they?)

Then, because it's lunchtime, you shuffle over to the food court to gather strength for the shopping to come (even though you don't need anything). The lines are long, but you finally decide on the $5.95 burger-fries-shake special and wolf most of it down. (Watch people in food courts. This is what they always do.) But in your hurry to shop you managed to down only $3.95 worth, leaving $2.00 of food literally on the table, $2.00 wasted.

After lunch you happen to notice that your favorite sweater, regularly $50, is on sale at two for the price of one. You can't wait to buy two in different colors, forgetting that you have three just like them at home ($50 wasted). After a purchase that saved you so much money, you now have a craving for yogurt. You get one scoop (a pathetic one at that) with sprinkles on top for the bargain price of $2.75. The same scoop at home runs about 30 cents, but of course you're not at home. Money evaporates in a hurry when you're having fun, doesn't it?

You get the picture. Waste is everywhere. Impulse buying at the checkout line. Shopping just for the "fun" of it. Purchasing things, finding out you don't need them, and failing to take them back. Charges for ATM withdrawals and deposits and using PIN numbers. The list goes on and on and on.

22 EASY WAYS TO WASTE LESS (SAVE MORE) MONEY

There are literally hundreds of ways people waste money, and there are just as many simple, powerful ways to eliminate that waste. Here are just a few Bill's teenage students thought of. You and your family probably can add to this list. (Later in this chapter, we'll give you tips for doing many of these things. For now, we just want to get you thinking about your habits.)

1. Don't go shopping just to shop. Shop only for things you need.
2. Use fresh foods. They're cheaper than frozen or prepared ones.
3. Shop the Internet for cheaper prices.
4. Buy a less expensive car than you can afford.
5. Avoid ATM machines. Save the fees.
6. Put pocket change into a jar at the end of each day.
7. Buy things you need on sale. Be alert to seasonal and special clearances.
8. Use a debit card instead of a credit card to avoid interest charges.
9. Pay off credit-card debt first, starting with the card with the highest rate.
10. Clip coupons for things you need.
11. Shop for bulk items at a Sam's Club or other discount warehouse.
12. Bank where there are no service charges.
13. Invest only in no-load mutual funds if you have to invest in funds at all.
14. Use discount instead of full-service brokers.
15. Have your local utility conduct a free energy audit to reduce your home energy costs.
16. Buy clothing at quality consignment shops such as Goodwill and the Junior League.
17. Shop around to reduce automobile and homeowner policy premiums.
18. Shop at discount stores, which usually are cheaper than department stores.
19. Attend matinee or twilight movies.
20. Always use a list when you shop.
21. Don't overpay your taxes and wait for a refund. You lose interest that way.
22. Don't purchase lottery tickets. (Maybe one or two a year is okay if you really have to.) They can become addictive.

BANK ON IT

NEVER SPEND YOUR MONEY BEFORE YOU HAVE IT.
Thomas Jefferson

BUDGETING: THE RIGHT WAY TO TAKE CHARGE OF YOUR MONEY

Someone once wrote, "A budget, like ants at a picnic, is universally unappealing." Who really wants to do it? *Budget* derives from the French word *bougette*, which is a "pouch or small bag with its contents." An expanded current definition is the annual statement of expected income and expenses.

People who attempt to budget and save for the long term often fail because they're too hard on themselves and their "plan" is much too restrictive. Having a budget or a financial plan doesn't mean you never go out and have fun. If you deny yourself everything, you'll quickly lose sight of the fact that there is only one point to saving: freeing yourself financially to enjoy life today and in the future. You should treat your money seriously, but not too seriously.

People in difficult financial shape often let fear prevent them from improving their situation. They're so worried about losing what little they have, they take no steps forward to get out of a financial hole. But there's no reason not to save some of your money and have fun with it too.

For most families the three most important financial "dreams" are educating children, having enough money to live comfortably in retirement, and securing good long-term health care. Other critical goals include fixing up their current homes and being able to afford fun vacations.

We prefer to call retirement "life after work" because retiring has connotations of being old and inactive, when the opposite is usually true.

BANK ON IT

THERE IS NO DIGNITY QUITE SO IMPRESSIVE,
AND NO INDEPENDENCE QUITE SO IMPORTANT,
AS LIVING WITHIN YOUR MEANS.
Calvin Coolidge

If a man or woman reaches age 60 to 65 in good health, the odds are very high that he or she will live at least another 20 years. One of the biggest problems older people in this country face is living a long, healthy life but not having enough money to travel and do whatever else they wish to do in their later years.

The typical married couple reaching age 65 has about $7000 in liquid assets in addition to Social Security benefits and possibly home ownership. At the rate you're spending money today, how long would $7000 last? Two months? Three months? Four months? We doubt it would be beyond four months if that long.

It's easy to see why so many people aren't financially prepared for the future. They don't save enough money and sometimes save nothing at all. All their income is spent to pay the grocer, mortgage company, auto dealer, department store, phone company, local utility, doctor, television repairperson, movie theater, video rental store—the list goes on and on. They spend every dollar they make. Sometimes they spend more than they make and borrow to make up the difference through home equity lines and a multitude of credit cards. They reason that one day they'll start to save some money as soon as they quit spending so much, but few really ever do it. It's a fantasy.

To be able to have money for your long-term financial needs, you've got to be able to save, and you can do it fairly easily without having to have a Ph.D. in personal finance. We promise you this is true. Let's get started.

It's time to prepare the family budget. But don't do it the old-fashioned, make-it-as-complicated-as-you-can way. Instead whip out a sheet of paper and across the top in **BIG BOLD** letters write "monthly household after-tax income." (The typical American family grosses about $40,000 a year. After taxes that number would be in the area of $32,000 per year, about $2700 a month.) Then write the numbers 1, 2, and 3 beneath with lines beside the numbers (see the following chart).

On line 1 write down a fixed percentage of your income to invest (we hope in *America's Finest Companies*®, as you'll learn in Chapter 5) for you and your family. Start with any percentage that's comfortable and resolve to up the percentage at least a little bit each year. The more you set aside today, the more you'll have in the future and the faster you'll get to where you want to be financially.

On line 2 write down a fixed percentage of money you're going to give to charity, a church, a synagogue, and/or other worthwhile activities. The children can and should be involved in this decision. It's the truth: The more you give, the more you get. (We'll provide some inspiring examples in Chapter 4.)

Monthly (After-tax Household Income)
$2,500

1. Money invested for the future (3%) $75 *Lines 1, 2 +3 are sacred*

2. Money to give to others (3%) $75 *Never make cuts*

3. Money for fun/vacations (3%) $75 *Only increases*

Subtotal $225

Net left to pay all bills $2,275

Less: mortgage/rent, utilities, groceries, various insurance (home, medical, car), clothes, furniture, home repairs, etc.

This category is where the waste is.

Make spending cuts here.

On line 3 write down an amount of "money for fun/vacation." Don't let your budget be constraining. Use it to set yourself free. If you don't plan to have some fun with your money, you probably won't.

Add lines 1, 2, and 3 and then subtract them from your monthly after-tax income. This is the amount of money you can spend each month for everything else, including utilities, groceries, insurance, and mortgage payments. If you're spending more than is left over, cut your spending here.

Never, ever reduce or cut out what you wrote down on lines 1, 2 and 3. That money is sacred. It's the most important money you have. You must treat it that way.

Americans who don't do well with their money use a different formula. When money comes in, they spend it on everybody they can think of, and if—this is a big if—there's any money left, they use it for themselves, for others, and to have some fun. Their dilemma is that there's never anything left because they don't plan for there to be.

If somebody says, "I'll try to do it," what are the odds he'll do it as compared with if he says, "I will do it"? You can't try to do anything. Either you do it or you don't. You can't try to save money. Either you do it or you don't. There is no in between about saving money and because there isn't, people get trapped. If you don't actually budget to save, it won't happen. But if you do budget, it will.

In the following pages we'll share specific tips for saving money. You'll discover how to spend less on major family events, ideas for saving when you buy a car, the best way to save for college, and other surprising strategies.

Beware of little expenses.
A small leak will sink a great ship.
—Benjamin Franklin

Do You Really Need an Expensive Wedding?

The average wedding in America today costs more than $22,000, and they aren't getting any cheaper.

Bar mitzvahs end up in the same category. A local meeting planner with Temple Beth El in Charlotte said that 9 out of 10 people she works with spend from $18,000 to $25,000. What do they get for that money? A weekend of activities including typically a Friday-night dinner for out-of-town guests, the religious service, a Saturday luncheon for all the guests and the congregation, a Saturday party for the child's friends, and maybe a Sunday brunch as an add-on.

We asked about having just one party for everybody or a dinner and a party without anything else. The meeting planner said that would get the cost to under $10,000, still a lot of money but a lot less than $18,000 to $25,000. She also chimed in, "Alan [her husband] and I will have to be creative for our two kids because we don't want to spend that kind of money."

A friend sent an e-mail in which she shared an article from the *Orlando Sentinel* about the quinceanera celebration (a kind of "sweet 15" party for Hispanic girls). The article said some families spend upward of $10,000 to $20,000 per girl per celebration.

For weddings the reception is the most expensive part, averaging around $8000 for 200 guests. Next is the engagement and wedding rings in the range of $3000 to $5000. Then there are the flowers, the invitations, bridesmaids' dresses, tuxedos for the men, the wedding dress itself (which can easily cost $2000 and more), paying the minister, a limousine for the bride and groom, alongside a long list of "other" expenses. Interestingly, the cost of the honeymoon is not included in the $22,000 total cost, so let's throw in another $5000 or so for that. After all, who wants to be a Scrooge about the honeymoon?

The old expression "the honeymoon's over" supposedly came from a couple experiencing rough times soon after they returned from their honeymoon. We think that's not true. It may have originated from all the headaches that accrue from the multitude of bills that pour in after the wedding's over and everyone is back to reality, particularly the parents of the bride and groom, who probably paid a lot of the bills if not all of them.

Several years ago one of our friend's daughters was getting married to a really nice young man. The father of the bride said, "Blakeley, my budget for your wedding is $15,000 and I won't put in a cent more. You and your beau can spend all of it or some of it and pocket the difference for your future. The choice is yours."

After several conversations between the bride-to-be and the groom-to-be, which naturally included the mothers-in-law-to-be, the couple decided to max out the wedding at $5000. They pruned the guest list significantly after realizing that a lot of the money for the formerly big affair would go to entertain a bunch of people who were almost strangers, at least to the bride and the groom. Thus, the $10,000 freed up was used toward a down payment for their new home. A check was presented to the happy newlyweds on their wedding day. What a nice present, wouldn't you agree?

We love this story. One, it's a slice from real life. Two, it points out how many times in life a major one-time expense can be pruned fairly easily with little pain and significant financial benefits. Another is funerals, which average more than $6100 nationwide, but we're not getting into that. Who wants to think about death in an otherwise fun book about you, your family, and your money?

Want to Earn Double-Digit Returns on Your Money?

You can do this by paying down your credit-card bills. The average family with credit cards owes more than $8000. At 18 percent a year interest, which in many cases is low, the interest alone is $1500 a year—$125 month. Translated, if you pay nothing but interest at 18 percent a year on $8000, the credit-card company gets $8000 in interest in less than 5.5 years (it has doubled its money), yet you still owe it the same $8000 you owed before.

What can you do if you're over your head in credit-card debt? First, shop for cards with a lower rate and shift balances to those cards. Second, go to a credit counselor to help you reduce payments. Third, call all your card companies and negotiate lower rates. You might be surprised at how cooperative they can be, especially if they think you may have trouble paying. Fourth, declare bankruptcy, but that is not a good choice, so don't do it.

Fifth, just spend less and pay off the credit cards, as much as you can and as often as you can. One word of caution: Millions of Americans have obtained home-equity lines of credit to pay off credit-card debt. Although the interest rate on a credit card is usually a lot higher, peo-

I had plastic surgery last week.
I cut up my credit cards.

HENNY YOUNGMAN

ple using that strategy probably overlook the fact that they are trading unsecured debt for debt backed by their homes.

If they find themselves unable to meet equity-line payments for even a few months, they could lose their residences. As one astute observer notes, "A home-equity loan serves only to cover up bad money management and buy consumers some time. Home-equity loans are a good idea only when combined with a detailed long-term financial plan." A hearty hurrah for such sage advice.

> *$1000 left to earn interest at 8 percent a year*
> *will grow to $23 quadrillion*
> *in 400 years, but the first hundred years are the hardest.*
> —Sidney Homer

A 529 Plan: The Finest Way to Pay for College

Enacted in 1996, 529 plans are named after a section of the Internal Revenue Service (IRS) code. There are two types: prepaid plans and savings plans. The principal difference is that prepaid plans lock in today's tuition rates and pay for tuition (excluding room and board) at any state's eligible colleges and universities. Savings plans, the ones we believe in, offer much more flexibility and can be used for anyone (including partnerships, charities, and trusts) who wants to save for another person's education. One major benefit is that high-income individuals and families are included and can get all the same benefits as those at lower income levels.

Account owners can contribute as much as $55,000 a year or $110,000 annually per married couple (per individual) without incurring the wrath of gift or estate taxes, assuming the money is said to have been paid over a five-year period (that is easy to do).

The state sponsors of the relatively new college 529 savings plans have increased the amount that can be saved in these plans. In 2001 most capped total contributions at $160,000 or less. Now the average contribution limit is $217,729 according to a *USA Today* computer analysis. Tennessee raised its contribution limit to $235,000 from $100,000, a 135 percent increase. Michigan boosted its plan to $235,000 from $125,000. Kansas almost doubled its maximum to $235,000 from $127,000. The highest total contribution we knew of as we went to press was $281,543 in Louisiana.

Many administrators of 529 plans initially based their limits on the cost of four years of education at the most expensive college in their state. That ensured they would remain within the IRS guidelines for the plans. But most now let participants use their savings at out-of-state schools. States have revised their limits to reflect the cost of attending the most expensive schools in the United States and have included the cost of graduate school.

College 529 plans increasingly are being promoted as an estate-planning device for wealthy grandparents. In 2003 individuals could give away up to $11,000 a person—$22,000 for a married couple—without triggering gift taxes. But if the money is contributed to a 529 plan, givers can compress five years' worth of gifts into one year. That means a couple could contribute up to $110,000 in 2003.

Money in these state-run plans (1) grows tax-deferred (federal always) and (2) is withdrawn tax-free if and only if the money is used for college expenses. In addition, more and more states exempt the money from their taxes and several even give a deduction for the initial contribution, in itself an extra benefit. Money in these plans can go toward tuition, room and board, books, transportation, and various other "legitimate" expenses.

These plans are offered in all states and almost always allow investing only in mutual funds, even though investment options seem to be growing rapidly. Some plans are a lot better than others. But they are changing rapidly and improving, and so it pays to do some research on your own if you want to use them. These plans allow parents (and grandparents too, as well as other relatives) to join virtually any state plan and use the funds accumulated for any college in America alongside a growing number of foreign institutions.

College is a big deal in many ways, and in particular in regard to expense at $100,000 and up for a four-year private college. What will college cost in 5, 10, 15 years? One estimate we saw was $250,000 in 18 years. Historically the cost of college has grown at about 6 percent a year, well above the rate of the inflation for the last two decades, and far faster than individual family incomes—before or after taxes— are rising.

Any contribution by a nonparent is treated for tax purposes as a gift. Grandparents can contribute $20,000 a year to as many grandchildren as they want without having to pay taxes. If they exceed that amount for any of the grandchildren, the contribution could be treated as if it were made over a five-year period. If the grandparents will end up dying with a taxable estate, this is one easy way to reduce the value of that estate.

One amazing feature of 529 plans is that the donor maintains control of the account and can change beneficiaries too. But there are many nuances to the various state plans, including varying investment fees, investment choices, and eligibility.

Until fairly recently the easiest way to stash money for college education was into a Uniform Transfers to Minors (UTMA) account, or Uniform Gifts to Minors (UGMA) account in some states. The tax breaks on these accounts aren't bad. In a regular custodial account the first $750 of interest income is tax-free until the child turns 14. The next $750 is taxed at the child's rate of 15 percent. Everything beyond that is taxed at the parents' rate, which can be as high as 39.1 percent. In a 529 savings plan earnings are completely tax-free. Vive la difference.

You can set aside huge amounts of money, in a lot of cases far more on an annual basis than all but a small percentage of families earn: more than $200,000. All this is good news. And in at least 32 states you now can transfer children's custodial accounts into 529 plans with no penalties.

However, there's another side to consider. Usually you get a small number of mutual funds in which to invest. It's hard to tell what kinds of funds in the various state plans will deliver what kinds of returns because these plans are relatively new. The *Wall Street Journal* singled out 10 major plan investments for 2001. The five best ranged from a –0.86 percent return to –6.28 percent, which beat "the market"; the worst ranged from –13.25 percent to –20.86 percent. Unfortunately, funds are about the only choice now, but perhaps that will change in the future and you can purchase stocks instead of funds in the plans you pick. Still, even with the problem of mutual funds, there are so many benefits to the 529 plans overall, they're hard to ignore.

A superb website to check out is www.savingforcollege.com, a "fantastic source of information on every state's college tuition savings plan," and www.collegesavings.com. Another is www.kiplinger.com, which has details on every state plan as well. If you want to check the ins and outs of securing financial aid for college, and believe us, there are a lot, go to www.financialaid.com.

Teach Your Children How to Save

At one of our wealth-building seminars in Washington, D.C., our sister-in-law Ellen told the story about how John D. Rockefeller, one of the wealthiest people in history, taught his children about the value of money. He required them to keep a weekly journal detailing where their money went. They also were required to save some and give some to others who needed it. If they failed to keep the journal up-to-date and/or didn't save and give, they lost a week's allowance.

We're not necessarily into journaling (although it's a sound idea), but we are big supporters of giving even young children allowances. They are family members, and all members should share in the total family income. Let us use our 14-year-old son as an example.

Will started getting an allowance at age five, which was equally divided into money he could spend, money he had to save and invest, and money he had to give to others (Sunday school). Today he gets $8 allowance a week and is able to earn additional money by mowing the lawn, blowing the driveway, and cleaning the pool from time to time. In a good week Will can earn as much as $35, which mounts up to $140 per month during the six or seven months when the grass is growing and the pool is open.

Here's a simple, creative way to help children of any age understand the value of money. You know the feeling. Sometimes there's just too much month at the end of the money yet your children "desperately need" a hot new pair of $165 sneakers, a sixth skateboard (the other five are out-of-date), $35 to go to the nearby amusement park for the day, a $75 polo shirt like all their friends have—the list goes on and on.

Although America has such abundance, we have as many problems dealing with money and children as any other nation has. On the one hand, we want our children to have nice things. On the other hand, we want them to spend money wisely and not waste it.

If this is a concern in your family, try this. The next time you pay monthly bills, let your children who are old enough write all the checks before you sign them. Hand them the stack of bills and a calculator with the net amount of your latest paycheck already programmed in. Each time a check is written, subtract that number from the figure before it. It's amazing how fast what seemed like a substantial initial amount is whittled away to little or nothing after all the bills are paid.

With younger children you can make a game of paying bills and still make a point. Get some Monopoly money or similar fake money that's equivalent to the amount of your monthly after-tax salary. Then spread all your bills over a large table so that none overlaps another. Let the children help you count the money to pay each bill and place that amount on top of it.

It won't take long before what started out as a large stack of money dwindles to a considerably smaller one. Even young children can appreciate something, in this case money, shrinking from larger to smaller.

BANK ON IT

YOU WANT TO KNOW IF YOU WILL BE RICH.
THE ANSWER IS, "CAN YOU SAVE MONEY?"
Andrew Carnegie

Start a Retirement Plan for Your Children

The massive power of compounding in high-quality companies is what Staton Institute member Ingo Schukraft was counting on for his 22-year-old daughter, Erika. Schukraft started a retirement portfolio for her with an initial $11,000 contribution, which Erika is funding with an additional several thousand dollars annually before finishing graduate school. After that she might stop adding to her nest egg. Based on the historical performance of *America's Finest Companies*®, our exclusive list of companies found in Chapter 5, Schukraft calculated that Erika's portfolio will be worth at least $4 million by the time she's 65.

Buying, Selling, or Refinancing a Home

Recent changes in tax law now allow a single taxpayer an exemption of $250,000 of profit from the sale of his or her home. That exemption doubles to $500,000 for a married couple. The bad news is that any profit beyond the exemption is taxed at a straight 20 percent federal rate.

The good news is that you can subtract all the money you or you and your spouse paid over the years for capital improvements while you occupied your home. Be sure to keep all receipts for capital improvements in case the Internal Revenue Service ever wants to know more.

Be sure to check your credit score. Having just refinanced our mortgage, we know how important a credit rating can be. You probably have heard of the FICO score, the one most lenders put the most credence into. This score is from the Fair Isaac Co., which a little more than a year ago started selling an individual's score for $12.95. They also have a useful calculator at www.myfico.com showing the average mortgage rate vis-à-vis your score. The higher your score, potentially the lower the mortgage rate. www.eloan.com gives your score away at no charge.

Both sites can help you figure out how to move your score higher, assuming it's low; that can save you money on interest charges for mortgages, insurance, credit cards, and bank loans. You also can contact the Institute of Consumer Financial Education at 619/239-1401 or visit its website at www.financial-education-icfe.org to learn more. It's a solid idea to check your credit report at least annually and correct any mistakes the bureaus have made (which can be legion). Even small mistakes such as a late credit-card payment or two will lower your score.

With the information above, you can find out what you need to do to move your credit rating to blue-chip status, unless, of course, it's already there.

> *Money makes money. And the money that money makes*
> *makes more money.*
> —Benjamin Franklin

Tips for Staying Cool and Reducing Energy Bills

Better home energy management is simple and inexpensive according to Duke Power (www.dukepower.com). The following tips can help customers reduce monthly power bills and make their homes more comfortable for years to come.

1. Make sure your central air-conditioning system or window unit is the proper size for the space it is intended to cool. Improperly sized units use more energy than necessary.
2. Remember that window air-conditioning units generally are not designed to cool more than one room. Clean or replace window-unit or central-air-conditioning system filters monthly. Dirty filters cause air conditioners to work harder and use more energy.
3. Check the weather stripping around doors and the caulking around windows. Properly sealed doors and windows help prevent warm outside air from entering the home.

4. Close blinds, shades, and drapes during the hottest part of the day to block the sun's heat. If you have a central air-conditioning system, do not close off unused rooms or shut air registers in rooms. The system will be less efficient and cost more to operate.

5. Make sure an outside air-conditioning unit or shrubbery, leaves, or other objects do not block your heat pump.

6. Set the thermostat on the highest comfortable setting. Just a few degrees less on your water heater and heating system, plus three or four degrees higher on your air conditioner, will whack 10 to 20 percent off your monthly electric and gas bills.

7. Place heat-producing appliances such as lamps and televisions away from the air-conditioning thermostat to prevent inaccurate temperature readings.

8. Make sure the attic is ventilated properly to relieve excess summer heat. Duke Power recommends 1 square foot of free area for every 150 square feet of total attic floor space.

9. In homes without air-conditioning systems use fans to draw cooler air inside during the night and circulate air throughout the home during the day. Fan blades should rotate clockwise in the summer months.

10. Save jobs that produce moisture—mopping, dishwashing, and washing clothes—for early morning or nighttime hours. The humidity from these activities can make homes uncomfortable. On hot days cook outdoors, use a microwave oven, or prepare cold meals to avoid excess heat in the kitchen.

Certainly there are lots of things in life that money won't buy,
but it's very funny—have you ever tried to buy them without money?
—Ogden Nash

Another Simple Way to Slash Home Energy Costs

Yogi Berra says, "You can see a lot just by listening." We were listening closely when a financial coaching client told us a little bit about his business. He was an energy specialist with our local electric utility, Duke Power.

At the beginning of the client's coaching session Bill asked, "Which is more efficient, the electric or gas heat pump?" The gas company says one thing, the electric company another. He responded, "Generally, neither. A combination electric-gas heat pump is often the best and most efficient." We didn't know there was such a combo. That's one we saw just by listening.

The other was that Duke, as do many other utilities, helps you pay for an inspection of your heating-cooling system, including all the ductwork. Mary called Duke Power and promptly made an appointment. More than likely your local gas and/or electric utility has a similar position.

Duke, like so many of its counterparts, offers a simple-to-follow energy audit that breaks down household costs for cooling, heating, lighting, and appliances. In addition, Duke will give you an instant report suggesting lots of ways to reduce your power bill. Even if you're not a Duke client and your local utility doesn't offer a similar service, you can use Duke's online report.

Within a week a contractor authorized by Duke came out and checked our 10-year-old system. Around noon they called with the bad news: We had the best heated and cooled crawl space they'd seen in a long time. Sixty percent of the output of our three-ton unit downstairs was leaking underneath the house. Twenty percent of the one-ton unit upstairs was doing the same thing.

"How much will it cost to repair?" we asked. "About $500," came the reply. We said, "Do it." Counting the inspection and the work, there was a total bill of around $800. Duke Power picked up nearly $300 of that.

We paid the balance of just over $500 and were happy to do it. No one wants to heat and cool under the house, least of all us. We expected to recover our investment in two years and from then on save at least $200 to $300 a year, every year, without spending another nickel. And that is exactly what we did.

If one phone call can snare this kind of return, we can't imagine why anyone wouldn't want to do it, can you? And if you own real estate besides your home, the same kind of inspection could save you a lot of money there too.

Energy-Saving Appliances

Compared with two to three generations ago, we're energy hogs. Around the turn of the twentieth century the few American homes with electricity might have had one or two sockets delivering 100 watts of power. In marked contrast, today it's easy for an American home to be using 4000 watts or more at a time, particularly on a hot day. We burn the power with microwaves, coffee makers, toasters, bread makers, electric toothbrushes, hair dryers, curling irons, televisions, radios and stereos, computers, hot tubs, and heated blankets in addition to heating and air-conditioning units. The U.S. Department of Energy said in 2001 that the average American household spent $1300 per year on energy. Cutting that by 10 percent amounts to saving $130. A 20 percent reduction is worth $260.

Maybe we shouldn't have been, but we were surprised to discover that a 1980 refrigerator costs about $110 a year to run versus a new energy-efficient model, which runs at roughly half that. Of course you have to pay for the new one to get these savings, and that may cost as much as $600 to $700 to get the maximum benefit.

When we were growing up, our grandparents and parents told us to turn off the lights when we left a room. That advice stands today. Turn off all the lights when you're not using them, and ditto for all appliances.

Become a Millionaire Just by Buying a Less Expensive Car

Bill will never forget giving a seminar several years ago in Atlanta to a group of elite insurance salespeople making high six-figure incomes. When the session was over, one of the attendees approached him and said, "If I ever come to one of your seminars with my wife, please don't use this example." Then Bill smiled at him and replied, "Why? Might it be because you drive a fancy automobile and she drives a clunker?" He sheepishly replied, "Yes."

In our opinion the American automobile is one of the greatest, if not the greatest, extravagances in the typical family's budget. Our observations over the years, along with the voluminous reading we do, tell us that far too many people are buying more car than they need or can afford or both.

It is very easy to accumulate a lot of money, as much as a million dollars and more, simply by buying a less-expensive car and investing the saved difference every five years. By the way, this works whether you buy the car or lease it, although there are some differences in the final amounts.

Let's say you purchase a car for $20,000 but could afford $30,000. You invest the $10,000 savings in a portfolio of *America's Finest Companies®* growing at the historical rate of 13 percent per year (see Chapter 5 for details on how to invest for you and your family).

You wait five years to buy another car. Assuming that prices rise 4 percent annually, the $20,000 vehicle will then cost $24,333. The $30,000 car will cost $36,500. The savings differential is $12,167. Invest that amount in your portfolio just as you did the $10,000 five years earlier and continue investing this way every five years until you reach age 65.

Following this strategy for 20 years saves you nearly $500,000. Following it for 30 years should push you past $1 million. Simply by buying a less-expensive car than you can afford and investing the difference, you can get to $1 million and more while you're still young enough to enjoy it, and without changing anything else about your overall lifestyle and spending habits.

The $1 Million Difference

1. Start with a $20,000 car rather than the one you could afford at $30,000.
2. Invest the initial difference at 13 percent with our worry-free methodology.
3. Assume car prices climb 4 percent annually.
4. Buy a new car every five years.
5. Invest the difference between the lower- and higher-priced cars each time.
6. Cash in at age 65.

How Much Will You Have?

1. If you begin at age 45, the invested difference will grow to $494,835.

2. If you begin at age 40, the invested difference will grow to $786,728.

3. If you begin at age 35, the invested difference will grow to $1,228,737.

Take the Hassle out of Buying a New Car

Do you know anyone who enjoys buying a new vehicle? We don't, and we hear it's often dreaded more than a trip to the dentist. Rather than fear something inevitable that has to occur every few years, here are a few simple ways to make this chore a lot more pleasurable, maybe almost fun.

There's a wonderful story about a woman in Atlanta (Bill saw the story on television) who trotted into the local Mercedes dealer, picked the exact car she wanted, named her price, and wrote a check to the salesman for that amount. When the salesman refused her offer because it "wouldn't be profitable for the dealer," she went home and logged on to the Internet. Within a few hours she located the exact car she wanted and at her price. Guess where the car was? It was at the same local dealer who had refused her initial offer.

There are a number of easy-to-navigate and very helpful websites that make the process as smooth as possible, and you don't have to buy through a site. Go to www.personalogic.com to help you locate your favorite make and model, along with free reviews of the cars and trucks suggested. We think www.auto.com and www.caranddriver.com also may help to narrow down your choices if you don't already know exactly what you want.

You should also visit local dealerships to check prices and see the types of vehicles you want. Don't buy on the first visit even if you find something you like a lot. Spec out the car and write down the price along with the features. Then leave and do this next step: Search a number of car-buying sites, including www.autobytel.com, www.carpoint.msn.com and www.autovantage.com.

At those sites you can type in what you want and see what offers come back, usually within 24 hours. In your negotiations (via e-mail) you can use free data from www.edmunds.com to find out what the dealer paid for the vehicles you like and then decide how much you're willing to pay above that.

Through the whole process you're in charge. You can visit dealerships to check things out because you know you won't have to do the buying face-to-face unless you want to. After all, the dealer knows a lot more about selling cars and trucks than you do about buying them. Working through the Internet puts you in control and makes the playing field much more level.

We get lots of valuable input and advice from readers of our weekly e-mail investment newsletter. This timeless idea came from a friend and reader in Memphis. It's about buying a car, new or used, another hassle-free way.

Linda H. wanted to purchase a new car without any of the haggling that seems to be a part of the process, and so she and her husband visited a few local dealers to look at some models and "kick the tires." (We don't know why anyone would do it, but kicking the tires seems to be important in the purchase of any vehicle, except perhaps a tank.)

After these visits, Linda sent the following fax to several local dealers. It read:

To: Dealer X

Date: 6/30/03

Re: I am going to purchase an automobile this week.

I will pay cash and do not wish to negotiate. If you want to submit a bid for a cash deal, to be consummated this week, you may return this fax to 123-4567. Specifications are on the attached bid sheets. I look forward to hearing from you.

There were two bid sheets in the fax. We're showing only the first one because the second was similar. Specifications: (we won't name the car), automatic, four-door, 1.8 liter, 16-valve, four-cylinder, floor mats, power locks/windows, intermittent wipers, cruise, tilt, AM/FM stereo cassette w/seek/scan, clock, air.

Color: Choice 1 Light Pebble, 2 White

Mileage: Can have from 0 to 10,000 miles

Price Submitted from Dealer _____

Location_____

Authorized Signature_____

Day Telephone #_____

Within hours she had several firm bids. Linda and her husband visited what they thought would be the best dealer, and her husband was able to secure an even better price than the best one they had gotten from the faxed responses.

No problems of any kind to get exactly the car they wanted. Sound too simple to be true? The most powerful ideas are often that way. Perhaps you don't want to pay cash up-front but would rather lease or finance. The same basic thinking applies.

One additional thought: When quotes come in, contact the dealer who came in second to see if it will match or beat the best offer, and if any others are close, include them too. If you got exactly what you want and it's been verified via fax, don't let the dealer change the deal. If it does, walk out and never go back.

Another wonderful resource is AAA of the Carolinas. One of the many fine things about AAA is that it offers an inexpensive ($50) car-buying service for members only. It won't try to sell you a vehicle but will try to find whatever you want at a price lower than the one the dealer quoted. You can save hundreds of dollars as we have done and avoid all the selling pressure from the dealers. Plus, you can have the exact vehicle you want delivered to your home or office.

Other benefits include comprehensive extended-warranty care that can reduce hefty repair bills or eliminate them completely. It also can be transferred to a new owner when you sell. Who can buy it? Only AAA members. (This is one of the few times we recommend an extended warranty on anything.)

Also check out AAA's vehicle-buying guide. They've done all the spadework for you. Well over 200 vehicles are rated, covering everything from safety to looks and comfort to performance and value. The guide is available even to nonmembers. Get a copy by phoning 800/231-0349.

Another simple and easy way to purchase a new vehicle is to do what our computer guru, Michael, did. He went onto the lot of the local dealer and wrote down the vehicle identification number and, using the sticker on the window, wrote down all the options and features of the vehicle he wanted. He then logged on to www.edmunds.com, which let him know tons of details about that vehicle including how long it had been on the lot and the dealer's cost. Michael was able to negotiate a super deal compared to what he would have gotten if he'd walked in and listened to the dealer's offer, which would have favored the dealer and not Michael.

Change Your Engine Oil Regularly

We have not seen an exact number but know that if you do virtually nothing else, changing your vehicle's oil regularly and often (2500 miles is an easy number to remember; so is 3000) can extend your car or truck's life expectancy by tens of thousands of miles while improving gas mileage along the way. Yet more and more vehicle manuals say that's not necessary. They say you can easily go 5000, 7500, or even 10,000 miles before an oil change. Don't believe it. Who writes these manuals? It's not the people who work on vehicles; it's the people who make and sell them. Big difference.

JiffyLube (and there are plenty of other chains as well) will get the job done quickly. They even follow up when it's time for another change. Don't waste a moment. If your oil hasn't been changed recently or, even worse, you don't know, make an oil change one of your priorities now. Get on a regular schedule and stick to it. You and your vehicle will be glad you did.

Are Your Tires Properly Inflated?

Checked your tires lately? A lot of people don't, especially younger drivers. Twenty-seven percent of passenger cars and 32 percent of sport utility vehicles (SUVs) and light trucks are driving around with at least one dangerously underinflated tire, according to a survey by the National Highway Traffic Safety Administration (NHTSA) released in late 2001.

Tires are considered underinflated if 8 pounds per square inch (psi)—or about 25 percent—or more below the manufacturer's recommended pressure. Most tires are considered adequately inflated at 32 psi.

Underinflated tires can lead to blowouts, which cause drivers to lose control and crash their vehicles. Underinflation also was blamed for the tread separation that plagued Firestone tires in dozens of accidents involving Ford Explorers. Even if it's not fatal, low tire pressure can mean poor vehicle handling, low fuel economy, and shorter tire life. A checklist for you:

1. Radial tires can appear to be inflated properly when they aren't. Check your tire pressure at least monthly.
2. Always check the pressure when tires are cold.
3. The correct front and rear tire pressures for your vehicle are printed on a sticker affixed to the vehicle's door or glove compartment and are listed in the owner's manual as well. The ideal pressure for your specific tires also is printed on the tire itself.

Learn More about Anything

Visit www.refdesk.com and quickly find out virtually anything you want to know on any subject. The amount of information is both tremendous and stupendous.

Best Time to Buy a New Computer

Personal computer (PC) prices typically fall when new technology hits the market. That decline is magnified after Christmas as stores look to push older models out to make room for the new. Only the most advanced gear is likely to stay pricey.

Before you set out to shop, however, you should figure out exactly what you want and how much you want to spend, whether its $399 or $1999.

"I tell everyone, 'Understand exactly what you're going to do with the computer, what you want, and what your budget is,'" said Stephen Baker of NPD Techworld, a firm that tracks personal computer sales on a weekly basis.

"'Follow the ads, check the manufacturers, choose who you want to buy it from. And then, when the price gets to where you want it, go ahead and buy,'" he advised.

For buyers who only want to send e-mails and do some Web shopping and aren't picky about how fast the computer is, January is an especially good time to buy.

Maybe a superfast microprocessor—the brains of the computer—is still on your wish list. Or perhaps you're craving gobs of computer memory for smooth editing of holiday videos. Maybe an extra-large hard drive to store a library of digital photos is your must-have.

With the latest technology, postholiday discounts may not be enough to get the price into your range. "The new stuff is never cheap. If you want the new stuff early, you have to pay a premium," Steve Kay said.

He advises buyers to avoid the latest technology and buy something that's been on the market for a few months. Or, he said, you can wait until the desired specification (spec) has been around for a while and drops in price.

Let's say you were shopping for a microprocessor with a speed of 3 gigahertz, or 3 billion cycles per second, one of the faster processors on the market. "If you wait four months or so, there will be a much higher-performing machine out and the 3-gigahertz one will be more shopworn. At that point you can get it for less," Kay says.

Worried that the machines marked for postholiday sales could be made with last year's DVD drive or microprocessors that limp along as you surf the Web? That happens less and less. And when it does, there is a way out, NPD's Baker said.

PC makers have been managing their inventory better, and so it's tough to buy a computer that is out-of-date, he said. And sometimes you don't need to buy the latest DVD drive or a huge hard drive; older components may be good enough for now, and new technology makes it much easier to replace them later on.

During the last six months almost all the PC makers have built easy-to-use high-speed connections such as USB 2.0 and FireWire into their machines; those connections make it easy to plug in a bigger hard drive or a different type of DVD drive down the road.

"Even if something has a smaller drive than what you wanted or what you think you're going to need in a year and half, you can probably buy what you want in a year and a half and just plug it in," Baker said.

Don't Buy Rental Insurance You Don't Need

Progressive Insurance Co. recently discovered that one-fifth of car renters buy insurance coverage 100 percent of the time from Hertz or another company and another fifth buy it at least some of the time. The reason is that they don't know whether they already have the coverage, which in many cases they do, through their own auto insurance and/or the credit card used to check out the car. Rental insurance ranges from a somewhat reasonable single-digit number to the outrageous in the range of $30 to $35, and that's per day.

Do you know whether you're already covered? If you don't, please find out. Frequent travelers can save several hundred dollars a year simply by eliminating vehicle-rental insurance they don't need.

Fly Me to the Moon and Back and Back and Back Again

American frequent fliers alone have accumulated enough free miles to make at least 19,000 round trips to the moon, approximately 9 trillion miles and counting. It seems obvious that this is hundreds and maybe thousands of times more miles than will ever be used. It's also obvious that with airlines in such dire straits and cutting back not only on flights but also on the number of "free" seats available, using points is becoming more difficult as each day passes and hundreds of thousands more miles enter the database.

Simple down-to-earth advice: if you got 'em, use 'em. Use 'em as fast as you can.

The Art of the Hotel Upgrade

When you're looking for a hotel room, try www.hotels.com. *Worth* magazine says, "Hotels.com holds so much sway that it can offer rooms when hoteliers' own booking agents have nothing to sell." www.expedia.com is worth a close look as well.

Now for the art of the hotel upgrade. We'd love to tell you we knew this, but we didn't. This helpful bit of information comes from Joel Widzer, a Ph.D. in industrial organization psychology, whatever that is. He says he's received more than 400 hotel upgrades everywhere he travels.

He calls more than one hotel directly and notes that he's trying to decide which one to go with. Supposedly, on one try a bidding war ensued and he got a $325 room for $149.

He asks the manager to note in the computer that he asked for an upgrade.

He praises the hotel front desk, gets the name of the person he's dealing with, and tells that person he'll send a note of praise if he or she is accommodating.

Healthy Habits Save You Money

We read in the local newspaper recently that roughly one-third of all vehicle-related deaths in our home county of Mecklenburg happen to people who don't wear their seat belts. We don't mean to point fingers at anyone, plus we have been guilty ourselves from time to time, but it seems really stupid to drive or ride in a motor vehicle without a seat harness. What an easy way to protect oneself against serious injury or save lives, yet millions of Americans apparently leave home without their seat belts buckled.

That small article got us to thinking about one of the major expenses facing almost all Americans, and that's medical care. A Stanford School of Medicine study in the 1980s found that people who follow these five simple rules will save at least $385 a year in medical bills in the first year. Since this study came out 20 or so years ago, it's likely that the savings today would be more than $500 annually. The five rules are as follows:

1. Don't smoke.
2. Limit alcohol.
3. Avoid saturated fat.
4. Exercise regularly.
5. Wear your seat belt.

The Stanford study observed that by obeying these five rules people over 65 save at least $4500 a year in medical costs. A simple example: Reducing alcoholic drinks from three to two per day saves $1000 or more annually, not including the cost of the alcohol and any mixers that go with it.

Compare that group of five rules with these seven:

1. Don't smoke cigarettes.
2. Use alcohol moderately or not at all.
3. Eat a nutritious breakfast every day.
4. Don't eat between meals.
5. Maintain your ideal weight.
6. Sleep seven or eight hours a night.
7. Exercise aerobically three or four times a week.

UCLA's School of Public Health says that keeping these seven good habits will add years to your life and help you feel younger too.

UCLA'S extensive research concluded that people who practiced no more than three of these healthy seven habits were two to three times more likely to die in any given year than were their counterparts who maintained six to seven. After observing over 7000 adults for five years, UCLA researchers discovered that 70-year-olds who followed all seven habits were as healthy as adults age 35 to 44 who maintained just three.

The Institute for Aerobics Research in Dallas released results of its extensive longevity study in 1989. It showed that moderate exercise such as a brisk 30-minute walk is almost as beneficial for longevity and overall good health as is, for example, running five miles a day. A number of other scientific studies that are much more recent concluded the same thing.

Despite the overwhelming evidence that modest amounts of exercise are very beneficial to maintaining good health, the Centers for Disease Control in Atlanta reported that 27 percent of Americans don't exercise at all and that obesity is becoming an American health plague. Apparently, more Americans of all ages are fatter than ever.

If you're not motivated to take care of yourself for any other reason, remember that poor health habits can be costly not just to your well-being but to your wallet.

Prevent Identity Theft

As MSNBC noted recently, "In the wrong hands, your ATM number can wreck your bank account. But a thief with your Social Security number can wreck your life." Most people protect their bank account numbers, credit-card numbers, and other valuable identifying data a lot better than they protect their Social Security numbers, which it seems everybody and his cousin ask for these days whether they need it or not.

Rule 1. Never—we repeat *never*—give your Social Security number to anyone unless it is absolutely necessary. And make sure that it is absolutely necessary.

Rule 2. Don't carry your Social Security number in your wallet, on your person, in your car, in your briefcase, or anyplace else someone can see it. Memorize it instead. If you ever think someone has stolen your Social Security number, immediately call the Federal Trade Commission's theft hot line, 1-877-IDtheft.

If the worst comes to pass, take this hard-won advice from a friend of ours:

"We've all heard horror stories about fraud that's committed using your name, address, Social Security number, credit, etc. Unfortunately, I have firsthand knowledge because my wallet was stolen last month. Within a week the thieves ordered an expensive monthly cell-phone package, applied for a VISA credit card, had a credit line approved to buy a Gateway computer, and received a PIN number from the DMV to change my driving record information online. And more.

"Here's some critical information to limit the damage in case this happens to you or someone you know. As everyone always advises, cancel your credit cards immediately. The key is having the toll-free numbers and your card numbers handy so that you know who to call. Keep those where you can find them easily (having to hunt for them is additional stress you *won't* need at that point).

"File a police report immediately in the jurisdiction where the card was stolen. This proves to credit providers you were diligent and is a first step toward an investigation (if there ever is one). But here's what is perhaps most important: Call the three national credit-reporting organizations immediately to place a fraud alert on your name and Social Security number.

"I had never heard of doing this until advised by a bank that called to tell me an application for credit was made over the Internet in my name. The alert means any company that checks your credit knows your information was stolen, and they have to contact you by phone to authorize new credit.

"By the time I was advised to do this—almost two weeks after the theft—all the damage had been done (there are records of all the credit checks initiated by the thieves' purchases, none of which I knew about before placing the alert). Since then no additional damage has been done, and the thieves threw my wallet away this weekend' (someone turned it in). It seems to have stopped them in their tracks."

Here are the key phone numbers:

Equifax: 1-800-525-6285
Experian: 1-800-301-7195
Trans Union: 1-800-680-7289
Social Security Administration fraud line: 1-800-269-0271

RESOURCES WE LIKE

Here we'll describe stores and services we have used and liked. We mention them simply because they provide good value.

Shopping

If you're looking for attractive things at discount prices, Ten Thousand Villages is worth a close look. They have a number of stores across America that sell high-quality, fairly traded handicrafts from around the world. One of the prettiest outside planter pots (made in Vietnam) we have ever seen came from there. It was cheaper than what we would have paid at similar stores and was better made.

The company works with disadvantaged artisans, pays fair prices for goods, and whenever possible works with volunteers in North American operations. Please check this group out. The items are first-rate, and you help people who really need it when you make a purchase. Go to http://www.villages.ca.

By the way, the coffees They sell are fantastic. They are cheaper than Starbucks and others, plus all the beans are grown with minimal damage to the world's rain forests.

The Lowest Long-Distance Rates

According to the April 2001 issue of *SmartMoney,* finding the lowest long-distance rates has become a lot easier. SmartPrice.com requests basic information such as your area code and calling habits and then spews out a list of low-price alternatives. This free service also provides quality ratings for phone companies from the Federal Communications Commission, and when better rates come along, it will send you an e-mail update automatically.

The Best Table in Town

Www.savvydiner.com is a free online reservation service that covers more than 30 major cities. Normally requests for tables, even at top restaurants, are confirmed within one hour. Cofounder Bill Matuszak says he often can make reservations for you at the finest tables even when you can't because "of the amount of business we send to restaurants." But even so, Matuszak suggests requesting a table at top restaurants at least two to three weeks in advance. He says it usually never pays to wait until the very last minute.

Become a Better Consumer

One reliable way to get your money to go farther is to subscribe to *Consumer Reports.* Lest you think we have any financial relationship with that organization, we can say emphatically that we do not.

We got the magazine years ago and for whatever reasons let the subscription slip. Recently we resubscribed for $26, which includes 11 regular monthly issues, the April auto issue, the current buying guide that's shipped immediately, and the next annual buying guide when it comes out (www.consumerreports.org).

Visit your favorite newsstand or bookstore and give it a look. You might find it worth subscribing to as well.

Avoid Financial Tangles

The American Institute for Economic Research (www.aier.com) was founded in 1933 at the bottom of the Great Depression. "The Institute's research is planned to help individuals protect their personal interests and those of the Nation," according to one of its publications. Interestingly, AIER represents "no fund, concentration of wealth, or other special interests" and "advertising is not accepted in its publications."

We have no relationship with this group except that we are members and for a paltry sum each year receive a lot of useful financial information. You can too. For example, we recently received a 156-page book called *How to Avoid Financial Tangles*. It doesn't have a great-looking cover, but inside is a lot of valuable, well-researched information. It was copyrighted in 1995 and revised in 2001 and is well worth poring through.

AIER is located in Great Barrington, Massachusetts 01230, and you can join for one year for only $59. Believe us, you'll get more than your money's worth.

The Best Way to Buy Legal Services

Most people never think about an attorney until they need one. In this litigious day and time attorneys can be more of an asset than ever before and can end up saving you hundreds if not thousands of dollars if you're ever the victim of a lawsuit. That's why we'd like to introduce you to a unique service called Pre-Paid Legal Services, which is a publicly owned company (symbol PPD on the New York Stock Exchange). In business since 1972, Pre-Paid Legal sells HMO-like insurance plans that give policyholders unlimited access to 30 provider law firms and 6000 referral attorneys in the 44 states where it is licensed to do business.

> *The best way for the majority of Americans to be able*
> *to assure themselves of legal assistance*
> *when they need it is through a prepaid legal plan.*
> —American Bar Association

A prepaid service plan is a type of insurance against legal catastrophe, but it is also an everyday service (like AAA) with which plan members can access professional legal help for advice, document review, will preparation, attorney letters and phone calls, and other preventive legal care.

Pre-Paid's plan costs just $25 a month for a family and includes but is not limited to the following: will preparation or updates, traffic tickets, business questions, review of contracts or other legal papers, buying or selling property, consumer and warranty issues, bankruptcy questions, lawsuits, and IRS audits. The average person is more likely to find himself or herself in court than in the hospital, yet most people have health insurance but no plan to solve legal problems. Half of all Americans will need an attorney's advice at least once during the next year. About half of those people will attempt to deal with the matter on their own—unsuccessfully.

Many big corporations, such as AT&T, American Express, and the Big Three automakers, offer this type of plan, which employees can use to handle mundane things such as house closings and problems with credit reports (which are a nuisance to try to get corrected). They've been available in Europe for decades but have only recently started to catch on in the States. Pre-Paid has a great plan for all businesses ranging from the largest to the smallest. Some corporations have found that their health-care costs went down dramatically after they set up an arrangement with Pre-Paid.

For more information, you can contact Victoria or Nik Koloff, the specialists who set up our family's plan. They will carefully explain the many benefits of the plan and answer all questions without trying to sell you anything or put you onto one of those annoying mailing lists you can never seem to get off. They have two direct lines: 615-302-1913 and 615-496-1882. You can e-mail them at thekoloffs@juno.com.

For Your Health

We get a free health e-mail newsletter you might want to look into. Log on to www.hsibaltimore.com and try it. There are several interesting topics each week that seem to be well researched.

Managing Your E-Mail

A recent issue of *On* magazine (www.onmagazine.com) explained how to eliminate much of the junk e-mail we all receive, also known as spam. They mentioned an outfit called the Spam Recycling Center, which forwards junk mail to antispam watchdogs. You can reach them by visiting spamrecycle@chooseyourmail.com.

Now, for that problem of switching your e-mail addresses and having others find you. The *Wall Street Journal* suggests this solution. Get your own Web address or domain name and you can keep the same e-mail destination for the rest of your life, for example, bill@billstaton.com and www.billstaton.com. Icann.org lists more than 150 accredited domain registrars, which charge from $5 to $25 or so per year.

The next step is to pick an "account manager" (type "free domain management tools" into your search engine). They automatically forward domain-name mail to your e-mail address with your Internet service provider. If you change ISPs, give the account manager the new address. Your domain address, which is where friends and business contacts send you mail, is unaffected.

The caveat: Some registrars with low annual rates levy additional service fees, and some are much better and easier to work with than others.

Help Spread Knowledge

The *Knowledge@Wharton* newsletter is a free service of the Wharton School (http://www.wharton.upenn.edu/) of the University of Pennsylvania, Bill's alma mater. This is a terrific e-mail newsletter, chock-full of helpful information about accounting, investing, marketing, and international business. It is easy to subscribe to, and it's free. Check it out. If you know people who might be interested in Wharton's research studies, the business school encourages you to spread the word.

OTHER SIMPLE WAYS TO EASILY SAVE MONEY

As a brief refresher from the beginning of this book, we remind you that there's an iron law of economics: savings = investment. Every penny, every nickel, every dime, every quarter and dollar saved is that much more money you have to invest wisely for yourself and your family. Plus there'll be more money for you to give away to help others.

We've already covered ways to save more money for some of the big financial events of life: buying a car; paying for your own or your children's weddings; bar or bat mitzvahs, and similar ceremonies; making your home efficient with an energy audit; and getting your kids through college without breaking your back or bank account. Now we're showing you more easy ways to add to your savings stockpile, again for the purpose of having even more funds to invest wisely for the future.

The following simple-to-do tidbits have been gleaned from personal experience, anecdotal evidence, various Internet websites, our newsletter subscribers, and a wide variety of articles we've read. When possible, we've tried to give you a reasonable range of the savings to be garnered from doing any one particular thing. Read them and use all that you can.

Big Savings Online

A number of websites, including www.overstock.com, www.bluefly. com, and www.smartbargains.com, offer a big variety of merchandise (books to electronics to jewelry to sweaters) that they claim is as much as 60 to 80 percent off retail.

Pocket Change

What do you do with your pocket change, all those loose coins and the occasional bill or two that seem to always fall out when you hang your pants or that jingle in your purses, wallets, and pocketbooks? A lot of people try to get rid of them whatever way they can. It may be difficult to believe, but we met a couple in 2001 who saved more than $1200 in less than two years by emptying their pockets every night before they went to bed and dumping the coins and bills into a drawer. One financial analyst estimates that this is an easy way for almost any couple to set aside $300 to $500 a year, which jibes with what the couple mentioned above told us. And there's another benefit: You won't even miss it. Go ahead. Get a jar or some other container and start today.

Avoid Extended Warranties

The rule of thumb here is to buy goods with solid warranties from companies you can trust that stand behind what they sell. Many service contracts generate about as much profit for certain companies as the underlying merchandise they peddle, and so naturally the companies push their warranties. Some credit cards offer extended protection beyond the original warranty. In the case of American Express it's one additional year after the warranty expires and at no extra charge.

Exercise Equipment

Got an exercise bike, treadmill, stair step, or another such device in your home that you're not using? You are not alone. Millions of your fellow Americans do as well. The airwaves are full of commercials and infomercials promoting this gizmo or that to build better abs or tighten buttocks. It seems each new device is easier to use and better than the one before, particularly if that refers to the one you already own. Exercise equipment is fine. We have no problem with that. Just don't spend hundreds of dollars on a piece of equipment that will never be used.

Cell Phones

The other day we saw a young woman driving a young child (we assume to school) while she was eating, smoking a cigarette, and talking on a cell phone. We can only assume she was driving with her feet because it didn't look like she had more than two hands. She reminded us that people use their cell phones a lot. Phone charges can mount up quickly, and at a high price too. If you have a cell phone, use it more judiciously and stay within your plan. You're sure to save several dozen dollars each month. And please be careful while talking while driving. A recent survey showed 25 percent of all vehicle accidents occur when someone is talking on the phone.

Look Around and You'll Find More Easy Ways to Save More Money

Taking lunch and soft drinks to work, canceling all the newspapers and magazines you don't really read, raising your insurance deductibles, and banking online are simple money-saving tools. Two other simple money-saving methods are buying generic brands whenever possible and using water filters for your faucets instead of buying bottled water, a lot of which comes out of the tap anyway.

Take It to the Top

At or near the top of the list of consumer complaints are three words: *poor customer service.* We would agree with that in spades. It seems to us that far too many businesses take all of us who buy from them for granted. Having said that, we want to praise some businesses, both big and small, with which we have had a superior experience. And we also want to share with you how to get a positive response when you have a complaint by "taking it to the top."

About six years ago, as a longtime customer of American Express, Bill had a beef he couldn't get resolved via the company's 800 number. He wrote a detailed letter to then CEO Harvey Golub and explained the situation courteously. (Being courteous and being rational are two keys to getting results.)

Within two weeks one of Mr. Golub's personal assistants called to say the problem had been taken care of. In addition, they were giving Bill a credit for $100 against our next bill. Happy we were. We had taken it to the top.

More recently our son ordered a four-pack of CD video games from amazon.com. Our family has been longtime customers and know they give terrific service. We are enamored with the way they treat customers. We looked at the games and decided they were inappropriate for Will, but we were way past their deadline for returning them for a 100 percent refund.

What to do? We decided to write CEO Jeff Bezos a letter and return the four CDs, saying they were too violent for young people and requesting a refund. We had paid $60 and got a nice letter saying our account had been credited $50. Since we were far past the deadline for returning merchandise, we felt great. We took it to the top.

One of the tremendous service experiences for our family has been with Wal-Mart. Never once has any of us been questioned about a return, even when he or she didn't have the receipt. Their people are courteous. They take you to where the merchandise you want can be found instead of mumbling something like "Go down aisle three, hang a left, take two steps, turn around, and look 47 degrees to your right." At least with Wal-Mart, so far we never had to take it to the top. But we know we could, and we also know they would be 100 percent on our side. After all, that's what Marshall Field meant when he said decades ago, "The customer is always right."

And now let's hear it for a small business: Coffman's Men's Wear, way down east in Greenville, North Carolina. Bill grew up just 13 miles away. His father, his brother, and he have dealt with George and his sons for longer than we care to remember. We probably spent enough in their stores to fund most, if not all, their retirement plan. You want service? Coffman's delivers. You want to return something? Never a question asked. Dissatisfied? Bring it back for full credit even if you've worn it for a while. Bill should know. He's done it more than once.

You don't have to put up with negative experiences when you shop. Take it to the top!

4

Give More

We make a living by what we get.
We make a life by what we give.
  —SIR WINSTON CHURCHILL

The *Wharton Alumni Magazine* published an article about Bill's fellow Whartonian Jon Huntsman, who has a sign in his office that reads, "The greatest exercise of the human heart is to reach down and lift another up." Huntsman runs the largest privately owned chemical company in the country, Huntsman Corp., with more than $5 billion in revenue and over 10,000 employees.

In 1998 Huntsman gave $40 million to the Wharton School, the largest gift ever made by an individual to any business school anywhere up to that time. That followed a gift of $100 million to the University of Utah to establish the Huntsman Cancer Institute to identify genetic factors that lead to cancer. In 1998 alone it is estimated that the Huntsman family gave away $70 million or more beyond the Wharton gift, and the Huntsmans continue to give. But even when he had very little, Jon Huntsman and his new bride gave about 20 percent of their monthly paycheck to help a needy family in the neighborhood.

Jon Huntsman is a prime example of someone who gives and gives, yet he reaps the reward of that giving, which includes personal satisfaction and additional monetary gains. Yes, that's right: A man and his family and his corporation continue to prosper because giving is at the top of their list of responsibilities. They recognize that you can't put anything into a container that's full, and so they continue to empty their monetary container only to find that it refills at an ever faster rate.

By giving you grow.
—Sir John Marks Templeton

Giving your time, talents, and money is one of the secrets to building wealth. Great men and women throughout the world have proved it over time. In the broadest sense sharing your wealth is an opportunity to change things for the better, including tremendous internal gratification from helping others. It really is true that what goes around comes around.

One of the greatest giving stories we ever heard was about the Olympic champion Charley Paddock, who won a gold medal in track and field in 1920. Paddock believed in himself and in the potential of others regardless of circumstances. While he was speaking at a high school commencement, a sickly, frail spindly-legged boy named James, age 13, the son of an Alabama sharecropper, said to the great champion, "I want to be a gold medal winner just like you."

Born in 1913, James Cleveland Owens, because of his ill health, could rarely if ever help his family pick cotton and tend to other chores. With few job opportunities and near starvation, the family eventually moved to Cleveland, Ohio, where James changed his name to J.C. When he entered grade school, the teacher mistakenly wrote down "Jesse" instead.

In 1935 J.C. traveled to Michigan with a bad back (so painful that his coach almost talked him out of attending) to participate in the annual Big Ten track and field championships. The *New York Times* reported that J.C.'s performance that day was "the greatest in track history." In under 45 minutes J.C. tied the world record for the 100-yard dash and then broke the world long-jump record and the world record for the 200-yard dash, and that wasn't all. He later set another world record in the 220-yard low hurdles, all in less than 60 minutes.

Of course you probably realize we're talking about the great Jesse Owens, a black American who won four Olympic gold medals the next year in Berlin with Adolf Hitler glaring at him. Owens set a long-jump record then that stood for 25 years.

But this is not the whole story, which expresses how giving never ends. Jesse Owens, a great champion and human being by anyone's standards, eventually went bankrupt. Before recovering, he inspired

BANK ON IT

Money-giving is a good criterion of a person's mental health. Generous people are rarely mentally ill people.

Dr. Karl Menninger

another young man just as he had been inspired as a youngster. That young man, Harrison "Bones" Dillard, tied Owens's Olympic record in the 100-yard dash in 1948.

Jesse Owens barely was recognized for his enormous struggles and achievements during much of his lifetime, but finally President Gerald Ford awarded him the Presidential Medal of Freedom in 1977. Two years after that President Jimmy Carter presented him with the Living Legend Award. Ten years after his death Jesse Owens was bestowed the Congressional Gold Medal, a true reflection of his talents and gifts to others.

THE MORE YOU GIVE, THE MORE YOU GET

Years ago as teenagers we read a wonderful story in *Guideposts* magazine about Joseph Colgate, founder of the forerunner of Colgate-Palmolive and Colgate University. Mr. Colgate's business was so successful, he quickly became a multimillionaire and decided he had far more money than he needed, and so he started giving it away.

He first gave away 10 percent of each year's income, but after he started, his income multiplied. He then upped the percentage to 15, and the same thing happened again. Next, he gave away 20 percent of his income, but money poured into his coffers like water through a broken dam. After studying his "problem," Colgate finally chose to turn his money over to a foundation and let others figure out what to do with it. Giving away his money created a giant hole, which was refilled with even more money than before.

In our business roles as money coaches and in our personal lives too, we operate under an amazingly simple formula. We mentioned it in the section on budgeting and will remind you again now:

100 percent of your monthly after-tax income
Less: money for you and your family's financial future
Less: money to give to causes and organizations you want to support
Less: money for fun
= money to pay all other expenses

Not only do we believe in paying ourselves first, we also believe in paying others first who need it. If we set aside 5 percent of our pretax income for ourselves, we also set aside 5 percent for charities, the church, organizations, and causes we believe in. Joseph Colgate proved this works. Many others have proved it too.

We receive freely when we give freely.
—Author Unknown

We're reminded of the story about a deep well with the purest, best-tasting water anyone for miles around had ever tasted. For generations the old well served all the descendants of a farming family and anyone else who wanted to partake of its goodness. Through drought after drought the well always provided all the water the farmer, his family, and his animals ever needed. Not once did it run low.

During the Great Depression hard times hit, and the farmer had to sell his farm and move. The property stayed empty and the well unused for many years until finally a new family bought it. Even though they came from another county, they knew the reputation of the old well and its water.

When the new family moved in and rushed to the well to sample its contents, they were shocked to find it completely dry. In great disbelief they stared at each other and realized the terrible investment they'd made by buying a farm with a dry well.

What they hadn't realized before they made the purchase was that a well needs to be used to keep the water flowing. The thousands of tiny rivulets that flow into the well's cavern will stop up just as blood will not circulate if veins and arteries become clogged through lack of movement or fat buildup.

And so it is with money. To do the most good, to help the most people, money must flow. This is a critical component of *Worry-Free Family Finances*. Money should not be hoarded as the Wall Street financier Hetty Green hoarded it.

Green could read the financial pages at age six. At age 30 she inherited her father's fortune and began trading on Wall Street with "bold audacity." It wasn't her looks but her fierce style that earned her the name "the witch of Wall Street."

The witch was so tightfisted, she wore only a black dress. To save soap she seldom washed it. Working alone on the first floor of a bank from which she coerced free space (probably because she owned it), Green lived the life of a pauper. She bought the *Wall Street Journal*, read it, and then resold it each day.

Despite her bizarre nature, she managed to marry and to bear two children. Her son, Ned, hurt himself sledding, and Hetty took him to a charity ward, where she was recognized as a multimillionaire who easily could afford a hospital. But she refused to pay, the wound became infected, and Ned's leg was amputated. Hetty Green died of a stroke in 1916 after arguing over the price of milk.

Clint Murchinson, Jr., the famous Texas wildcatter, had the right attitude about money: "Money is like manure. If you spread it around, it does a lot of good. But if you pile it up in one place, it stinks like hell."

James Redfield, the author of *The Celestine Prophecy*, also had the right attitude. His book sold more than 3 million copies despite the fact that the plot was called "flaky" and all other sorts of unflattering names.

In a fall 1994 interview Redfield said that when you view money as a scarce resource, you are locked into a scarcity mentality: "No matter how tight money is for you, if you don't open your hand and make it available, it'll be hard for you to get more. When you give, you create a void [like the old well] that is filled again. And [like Joseph Colgate] you always receive much more."

Redfield self-published 3000 copies of his best-seller and gave up his therapy practice, and he and his wife traveled across the Southeast giving away copies of the book. He sold 150,000 books that way before cutting a deal with Warner Books. Redfield made so much money so quickly that he and his wife set up a foundation to get rid of it.

He who sows sparingly will also reap sparingly,
and he who sows bountifully will also reap bountifully,
for God loves a cheerful giver.
—2 Corinthians 9:6–7

A prudent farmer doesn't dispose of his or her entire crop but always sets aside some of the grain for seed. When you give a certain percentage of your income, alongside your time and skills, you can consider this "seed" for another harvest. If you don't plant tomatoes, none will come up. If you don't fertilize your lawn, you know what it will look like.

Perhaps the best result of giving to others is that is brings a true sense of joy, accomplishment, and peace. In an uncertain world, isn't that feeling worth everything? Is there any greater gift than to help others?

We have a theory that good things, often unexpectedly great things, happen when people with a giving attitude "empty their glass." Only a completely empty glass can be totally replenished. One of Jesus' most famous parables is about the poor woman who gave her last two coins to help others. She trusted that even though she had no money after making the gift, her needs would be met. And we find that's true with giving in our lives as well.

We gladly give away our expertise to people who can't afford it without asking anything in return. The more we give, the more we are rewarded, frequently in ways we never anticipated. The saying that what goes around comes around is really true. We are all part of a giant circle, some 6.5 billion of us, and each one has a part to play. Every person has a way to serve.

Serving is what being human is all about. To serve is to give. The more you give, the more you get. The hand that gives, gathers.

Giving is far more important than getting, and those who give freely
will experience the return on their generosity.
—Sir John Marks Templeton

THE SACRIFICE DIET

Our Tennessee friend Dr. Winn Henderson helps people realize their true purpose in life through his writings, personal counseling, and hands-on seminars. He recently came up with a terrifically simple idea to lose weight while giving to others at the same time. While meditating one morning, as he typically does several times a day, Winn asked himself, Is there a way to transfer weight from someone who has too much to someone who has too little without it costing a single penny?

As a counselor with medical training, Winn knows that obesity is perhaps the number one national health problem, yet he also knows that millions of people, not only in this country but also around the world, are starving to death. He has written a little booklet entitled *The Sacrifice Diet* that explains the whole concept in greater detail. Before we go on, let's explain that the historical definition of *sacrifice* is "to give up something of value for the sake of something of greater value." It does not necessarily mean penalizing yourself.

In Winn's concept an overweight person gives up one or two items a day that aren't healthy. Two soft drinks comes to mind. Almost everywhere they're at least $1.00 a can in a vending machine, sometimes $1.25 or more. Let's say a person consumes four soft drinks a day at work. That's an extra 500 to 600 calories the body doesn't need. Now let's suppose this same person gives up two of the four drinks a day, saves $2.00 to $2.50, also saves some 250 to 300 calories, and gives that money to someone or some organization that needs it.

By making such a simple "sacrifice" anyone can, without harming himself or herself or anyone else, shed needless calories (save) and benefit others simultaneously (give). There are 3500 calories in a pound. Giving up two soft drinks a day would save at least 250 calories each 24-hour period. Translated, that's a loss of 1 pound every 14 days, 2 pounds per month, 24 pounds each year. Winn points out that that if just one in 25 Americans did this, it would amount to nearly $400 million annually to feed the starving.

First, health would improve because less sugar would be consumed. Second, the money freed up would amount to $500 or more to give to others, satisfying the wealth-building principle to give more. In addition,

The Most

The most destructive habit—worry
The greatest joy—giving
The greatest loss—loss of self-respect
The most satisfying work—helping others
The ugliest personality trait—selfishness
The most endangered species—dedicated leaders
The greatest natural resource—our youth
The greatest "shot in the arm"—encouragement
The greatest problem to overcome—fear
The most effective sleeping pill—peace of mind
The most crippling failure—excuses
The most powerful force in life—love
The most dangerous pariah—a gossiper
The world's most incredible computer—the brain
The worst thing to be without—hope
The deadliest weapon—the tongue
The two most power-filled words—"I can"
The greatest asset—faith
The most worthless emotion—self-pity
The most beautiful attire—a smile
The most prized possession—integrity
The most powerful channel of communication—prayer
The most contagious spirit—enthusiasm

as health improves and weight slowly but surely falls off, one of the other wealth-building principles comes into play: save more. In this case the saving more is about saving and improving your health, thus cutting long-run medical costs and maybe extending your life span while doing it.

Lest we hear from the Soft Drink Association, if there is one, we are not attacking soft drinks or any other food or beverage. Rather, we are suggesting that you and your family take a simple look at your caloric intake. If you want to lose a few or even a lot of pounds and benefit others too, this is a great way to do it. To lose a pound a week, consume 500 calories fewer per day. To lose a pound every other week, it's 250 a day. A pound a month is just 120 calories less a day, far less than are in four pieces of bacon, one bagel, a bean burrito, two slices of plain bread, a candy bar, or one slice of cheese.

In making this simple sacrifice, be sure to put the money you're not spending into a jar or another container. Then, at the end of each month, you can write a check for that amount to give to your favorite charity. You'll feel good about giving and be slimmer too.

TURNING YOUR CHILDREN INTO GIVERS AND INVESTORS WILL MAKE THEM MULTIMILLIONAIRES IN THE PROCESS

The Greek word *oikonomikos* is the root for both *economics* and another word in common usage, *coin*. Coins or metallic money began with bronze ingots in the form of cattle around 2000 B.C., followed by bean-shaped ingots roughly 1200 years later. The first modern coins appeared in Lydia circa 600 B.C. The Lydians began manufacturing the type of coin we use today—round and flat with images and values printed on the surface.

Kids, especially younger ones, love coins of all shapes and sizes even if they're not in U.S. denominations. Yours probably do too. When our son Will was seven, we wanted him to learn more about money other than just by accumulating it. We wanted him to be a good steward of his money as well.

At that time he received an allowance of $1.00 per day and was required to complete certain duties, such as feeding the pets, making his bed, and keeping his room straight. Will came up a few other things on his own.

As we emphasize over and over in these pages, the giving of time and money is an important piece, perhaps the most important piece, of *Worry-Free Family Finances* because it means so much and, we believe, pays off in the long run, not only in satisfaction but also monetarily. But how do you encourage giving in young children, and how do you inspire them to invest properly for their future?

Funny how a dollar can look so big when you take it to church and so small when you take it to the store.
FRANK CLARK

Will had to put his money into three different places. One-third went into his wallet to spend as he pleased. The second third went into a plastic bank in his room for giving: Indian Guides' monthly "wampum" and Sunday school, for example. The last third has built steadily and is now in both a bank savings account drawing interest and a stock portfolio Will picked when he was in second grade.

The millionaire part of this is that Will, with money he had been given, earned, and saved, started investing at age seven with a little more than $3000. Our rule for each of our four children is that whether you are given money or earn it, if you place that money into your stock portfolio, we'll match it dollar for dollar. Who wouldn't love such a deal? The children double their money right off the bat, plus parents, grandparents, aunts, and uncles all like it too because it means monetary gifts to the children won't be wasted. Those dollars will be invested wisely for the future.

Let's take a look at the example above. Will Staton starts with $3000 at age seven. He adds $50 a month that is invested wisely (as you will learn later), and the money grows at its historical rate of 13 percent each year. When he starts college, the amount is $14,400. With a continuing $50 per month addition, the amount will grow to $56,700 at age 30, $193,400 at age 40, $657,600 at age 50, and more than $2 million at age 60.

Please keep in mind that the initial investment amount was $3000 and that the monthly contribution was only $50 and was never increased. Besides the first $3000, roughly $32,000 more was invested, spread evenly over the next 53 years. And it multiplied to more than $2 million without taking taxes into consideration. Even with taxes at a high rate, that would be far more than most Americans have when they're 60.

Einstein was right when he said, "Compounding is mankind's greatest invention because it allows for the reliable, systematic accumulation of wealth." Will is putting humanity's greatest invention to good use for himself and for others. You and your family can do it too.

INSPIRING STORIES OF GIVING

Need more inspiration? Enjoy the following stories of giving and discover the unexpected benefits to those who gave.

Capt. P. W. Brown, FDNY

Former mayor of New York Rudy Giuliani eulogized Captain Patrick W. Brown (Patty), a decorated Marine who served two tours in Vietnam, on what would have been his forty-ninth birthday, shortly after the firefighter's death on September 11, 2001. Giuliani said Patty was a "legend" in the life of the Fire Department of New York. Patty earned more than 20 awards for valor yet remained humble throughout his brief career. And he gave and gave. For example, Captain Patty donated whatever monetary awards he earned to charities and also taught karate to the blind.

Patty Brown and 11 of his fire crew died when terrorists destroyed the World Trade Center. He and they gave the ultimate gift: the loss of their own lives to save others.

Oseola McCarty

The September 1996 issue of *Guideposts* magazine featured an article titled "Set Aside a Portion" about a black lady named "Miss Oseola" McCarty from Hattiesburg, Mississippi, whose philosophy was, "I would always keep up my church giving. Over the years God showed me how to spend a certain portion on this, how to spend a certain portion on that, and how to save the rest. It must have been him because nobody else showed me."

She grew up poor and had few of life's finer things, yet she read the Bible so much that "it got so tattered from use, I had to tape it up to keep the pages in. At the bank one day they asked me where I wanted my money to go when I passed on."

She told them, "I want to help some child go to college. I'm going to give my money to the University of Southern Mississippi so deserving children can get a good education." Her banker said, "Miss Oseola, that means you'll be giving the school a hundred and fifty thousand dollars."

In later years Miss Oseola was invited to visit the president and awarded the Presidential Citizens Medal. The laundress who gave scholarships to needy students was a giver all her life. We can't think of anyone who's ever looked happier than she looked in the photo we saw of her.

Sir James Barrie

We bet you don't know who wrote the classic *Peter Pan*. Give up? It was Sir James Barrie in the late 1920s. Just before the onset of the Great Depression Sir James announced that all the royalties from his monumental work would go to a certain London children's hospital. He said that the amount of his gifts would never be revealed, although today it is perceived to be one of the largest gifts of its time.

Helena Houston

In early 2001 Helena Gabriel Houston, a graduate of the University of North Carolina at Greensboro who taught fourth grade in Charlotte, North Carolina, for more than four decades, announced a $1.3 million gift to her college alma mater. That's the same school that lent her money so that she could attend.

A lady who grew up poor, Ms. Houston gave birth to a scholarship fund for 8 to 12 students each year who wish to become teachers. She was called a "straight shooter with a sharp memory" who bought two shares of the old Reynolds Tobacco in 1933, which in turn spurred her to a "lifelong fascination" with the stock market that she shared with her late husband.

They were not big spenders but were big savers and big givers instead. They gave away most of their money during their lifetimes. At the retirement home where Ms. Houston now resides, the staff says that she has never stopped teaching others. What a monument to her life!

Nootka Chief Maquinna

Nootka Chief Maquinna, who welcomed Captain James Cook and his men when they berthed at Vancouver Island in 1778, said: "Once I was in Victoria, and I saw a very large house. They told me it was a bank, and that the white men place their money there to be taken care of, and that by and by they got it back, with interest.

"We are Indians, and we have no such bank, but when we have plenty of money or blankets, we give them away to other chiefs and people, and by and by they return them, with interest, and our hearts feel good. Our way of giving is our bank."

Paul Newman

Over 20 years ago Paul Newman started a little company to market his homemade salad dressing. Since then he has donated every penny of the profits to over 2,000 charities, an amount that now totals more than 12.5 billion pennies; in dollars that's in excess of $125 million. Now he's into Fig Newmans, a variety of sauces, and various other products. Meanwhile, his company gives all the profits away. Newman doesn't see what he does as philanthropy. Instead, he says, it's an "investment in a community." Who says pennies don't mount up?

Do a Good Turn Daily

Do you believe that a good turn always comes back to the doer? We certainly do. Our son Will is a Boy Scout with the rank of Star on his way to the ultimate, the Eagle Award. The Boy Scout motto is "Do a good turn daily."

At age 11 John Kossuch saved another boy's life by pushing him out of the way of an out-of-control car. John received a certificate of heroism from the Boy Scouts of America, and his story was recounted in *Boys' Life* magazine in 1960.

Forty years later, in 1999, Kossuch, by then an assistant scoutmaster and a Scouting volunteer for many years, and his Eagle Scout son Ryan were shoveling snow from their driveway in frigid weather.

Feeling a little tired, the elder Kossuch went inside to get coffee and passed out in the kitchen. Actually, he didn't faint. Kossuch stopped breathing.

His wife immediately called 911 and yelled for Ryan, who rushed inside and quickly began cardiopulmonary resuscitation (CPR). When the rescue squad got there, they had to shock Kossuch's heart in order to start it beating again. Kossuch had heart surgery, and everything turned out fine. For his skillful action and heroism—like father, like son—Ryan also was given a heroism award.

This story has particular meaning for our family. All six of us traveled to eastern North Carolina for Bill's father's eightieth birthday in February 1992, an event at which roughly 200 people were expected to attend. Shortly after noon on that quiet Sunday and two hours before the shindig was to begin, Gracie, our oldest daughter, who was then 12, collapsed, and began to shake and turn blue.

Bill dashed in from an adjoining room and, with his sister-in-law Anne, began to administer CPR. We knew Gracie had a heart arrhythmia, for which she was taking medication, but we had no clue that she would ever go into fibrillation, also known as sudden cardiac death. Neither did her doctor.

Thanks to Bill's Boy Scout training in lifesaving techniques, Gracie's life was saved. Today she's a healthy thriving 25-year-old manager of an art gallery in La Jolla, California.

According to medical specialists, an estimated 300,000-plus Americans might be saved each year if someone standing nearby knew how to administer CPR, which is taught (along with the Heimlich maneuver) by the Red Cross, medical-emergency services, and a host of other organizations virtually everywhere. We should know. Bill has used CPR on others twice and the Heimlich maneuver on three other occasions. By learning both of these techniques, you may be able to save the life of someone as well.

There are so many simple ways to give. Spending time with family and friends is certainly a key one, as are giving blood and working in churches, synagogues, and other places. The list of organizations needing capable help seems endless.

J.L. Turner

Although corporate America and its leadership are not cited frequently for works of giving, we are familiar with dozens of examples among the companies we know quite well. One that stands out is Dollar General Corp. based in Goodlettsville, Tennessee. Dollar General has more than 5500 self-service discount stores primarily in the South and generates in excess of $6 billion a year in sales.

Some years ago, as we were studying the company for a potential investment, Dollar General sent (along with the usual financial stuff) a small brochure called "The Dollar General GED and Learn-to-Read Information Program." Along with it was a plastic business-size card. Let's start with the card.

On one side the company says its mission is "SERVING OTHERS!— A Better Life for our customers. A Superior Investment for our shareholders. A Partnership in Total Development with our employees." On the flip side are the corporate values statements:

We believe in building our company with persons who:
have a living commitment to moral integrity;
have an enthusiastic sense of mission;
humor and mature assessment of themselves;
model total development in their lives;
respect the creative potential of others.

We believe in leadership, which results in team creativity and prompt decision making close to the action. We believe in hard work; we also believe in the dignity of work and in the dignity of every person. We believe that productivity is attained by emphasizing strengths in a positive environment, not by dwelling on weaknesses in an environment of guilt or blame. We believe that any success is short-lived if it does not involve mutual gain.

Dollar General's simple yellow brochure tells the story of J.L. Turner, who was in third grade when his father was killed at a Saturday night wrestling match in Tennessee. J.L. had to quit school to help man the family farm and support his mother, brothers, and sisters. J.L. never made it back to school but later started the Dollar General chain alongside his son Cal.

As a result of J.L.'s lack of education, company management has always been aware of the problems families face when members don't get a thorough education. The brochure notes, "We understand, first hand, the kinds of problems children and families sometimes face. But we also want you to know the power, the joy, and the self-esteem education can bring. There are local agencies and volunteers where you live who also understand and want to help. Whenever you decide you're ready to learn something more, Dollar General would like to help, too.

"Sometimes one of the hardest things to do is to find out where to go to get help. For that reason, we have made all 3,000 plus Dollar General Stores in 24 states the place where anyone can go to learn to read; where to take the GED classes and the GED test: or where to sign up to become a tutor for someone who wants to learn to read."

Charles Feeney

We bet you never heard of Charles Feeney. We hadn't either until we learned about his story a few years back. Feeney was a billionaire who didn't own a home or a car or even a fancy watch. In New York City he rode the subway, he never flew first class, and he did his own grocery shopping with his wife.

According to Maureen Dowd of the *New York Times* (November 30, 1997), Feeney was a dedicated giver because "you can only wear one pair of shoes at a time." *Irish American* magazine honored Charles Feeney at the famous 21 Club in New York City when he was 66 by which time he had given away more than $600 million.

When Dowd penned the article, she wrote, "The *American Benefactor* magazine says Feeney may soon become the greatest American giver of all time," a man who happily dropped off the Forbes 400 list of wealthiest American people and families because of the size of his gifts. A smallish man with a gleam in his eye, he was pretty much nondescript if you scanned around any room where he was present.

When the 21 Club festivities ended, Dowd said, the corporate chieftains in attendance climbed into their limos. Feeney, wearing an "old gray raincoat and Irish tweed cap," left on foot.

The Gift from a Little Girl That Multiplied

A sobbing little girl stood near a small church from which she had been turned away because the church was too crowded. "I can't go to Sunday school," she sobbed to the pastor as he walked by.

Seeing her shabby, unkempt appearance, the pastor guessed the reason and, taking her by the hand, led her inside and found her a place in the Sunday school class. The child was so touched that she went to bed that night thinking of the children who have no place to worship.

Some two years later this child lay dead in a poor tenement building. Her parents summoned the kindhearted pastor who had befriended their daughter to handle the final arrangements. As her poor little body was being moved, a worn and crumpled purse was discovered, one that seemed to have been rummaged from a trash dump. Inside was 57 cents and a scribbled note that read, "This is to help build the little church bigger so more children can go to Sunday school."

When the pastor tearfully read the note, he knew instantly what he would do. Carrying the shriveled piece of paper and the cracked red pocketbook to his pulpit, he shared the story of the child's unselfish love and devotion. He challenged his church deacons to get busy and raise enough money for a larger building.

A newspaper picked up the story and published it, and that story was read by a realtor who offered the church a parcel of land worth thousands of dollars. When he was told that the church didn't have much money, he sold it to them for 57 cents. Church members then began to give and give, with the contributions growing larger. Checks came in from far and wide.

Within five years the little girl's gift, worth less than six dimes, had increased to more than $250,000, a huge sum for a time roughly 100 years ago. Her unselfish love had returned big dividends.

Today Temple Baptist Church in Philadelphia seats more than 3000 people. The City of Brotherly Love also is home to Temple University and Good Samaritan Hospital. In one of the rooms of the church's Sunday school building is a picture of the little girl whose gift of 57 cents started it all. Alongside it is a portrait of her kind pastor, Dr. Russell H. Conwell, the author of *Acres of Diamonds*.

Dick Thigpen

Attorney Richard "Dick" Thigpen lives in Charlotte and was 63 when President Kennedy was assassinated. In a fine interview with Dannye Romine Powell in the *Charlotte Observer* (May 9, 2000), Thigpen said he had worked all his life as far back as he could remember (which was a very long way) and never "wasted time worrying about what I didn't have."

A scholarship graduate of what is now Duke University, Thigpen organized a small law firm in Charlotte just after the Great Depression ended. He described our "Queen City" as a "town that was just waking up." He added a few gems well worth noting, especially about the three wealth-building cornerstones of this book: save more, give more, invest wisely.

He said, "Most people are lazy. They are mediocre in their desires and satisfied with bread and butter and a place to sleep." Advice for young people? "They should learn all they can. Earn all they can. Do all they can. Save all they can. Give all they can—some people don't make room for any blessing to come in to them. When I started work, I resolved to tithe. I discovered I could do more with 90 percent that I used to do with 100 percent."

Columnist Powell retorted, "Who's he kidding? Richard Thigpen could do more with 10 percent than most of us with 150."

What a Christmas Present!

Our friend Bailey Swertfeger from the eastern part of the state sent a nice little note about how he and his wife and a group of friends give each Christmas. Some years ago they decided to pass up holiday cards and gifts to each other and instead celebrate together over a dinner at one of the couples' homes. Each twosome contributes a dish and a check to a particular charity or another good cause such as a needy student. In the year we first heard about this the group gave away $2000. That has gone up every year since.

THE TAX BENEFITS OF GIVING

There are multiple tax benefits to giving. Gifts of cash, stocks, and bonds reduce the size of your taxable estate and can provide you and your family with annual deductions against taxable income. Things you do for others that are more indirect also can be deducted from your annual income tax if you abide by the law and don't make outrageous assumptions (used clothing, furniture, etc.). In general, the higher your and your family's income level is, the more itemized deductions will benefit you in tax savings.

For example, for driving to and from volunteer work in your own vehicle you're allowed to deduct 14 cents per mile along with any tolls and parking expenses. For public transportation, including buses and subways, you can take off 100 percent of the fare. Assorted expenses such as traveling on a mission trip with your civic or church group and helping to build a house for Habitat for Humanity can be deducted as well.

There are caveats. If an item such as a car, jewelry, or a painting worth in excess of $5000 is given, an independent appraisal is required. For other used clothing, old computers, and the like, you are supposed to render a conservative valuation of what they are worth. Note the word *conservative*. It is better to be too low than too high.

A rule of thumb is that the more documentation you have of what your gifts of cash and equivalents, travel, goods, and services are actually worth, the better off you are. IRS publications 526 and 561 are the "official" say-so on charitable deductions. For no-cost information you can call 877-829-5500 or visit at www.irs.gov/prod/forms_pubs.

Gifts to Children and Grandchildren

Thanks to federal tax laws, you can increase—in some cases dramatically—the value of appreciated securities by giving them to your children or grandchildren, lowering capital-gains taxes as much as 50 percent.

To avoid gift taxes you must limit your annual gifts to children and grandchildren (or any other persons you choose) to $11,000 per year or $22,000 for a joint gift from you and your spouse.

The easiest way to give appreciated assets to minors under age 18 is to transfer them into a custodial account. It's a simple process, and most brokers and mutual fund companies won't charge a fee. However, some-

---

BANK ON IT

THE CAPITALIST SYSTEM DOES NOT GUARANTEE THAT
EVERYBODY WILL BECOME RICH, BUT IT GUARANTEES
THAT ANYBODY CAN BECOME RICH.

Raul R. de Sales

---

times a minimum amount is required to open the account and avoid maintenance fees.

With this account you have no control over how the assets are spent. When the children or grandchildren come of age, they can squander the money if they want to or do anything else they please.

One solution is to set up a Crummey trust, named for D. Clifford Crummey, who waged war against the IRS in 1968 and won after they challenged his right to give money to his grandson by using this technique.

The trust works like this: You put money into a trust written to give the recipient the temporary right to withdraw the money, usually for 30 days. The recipient, of course, doesn't make the withdrawal, knowing that if she does, this is the last gift she'll get from you. After the 30 days are up, her right to the money expires until some point in the future that you have specified, such as when she turns 25 or 30.

If you don't set up a trust, when you give the appreciated securities, be sure to indicate if you want the child to cash in shares and take advantage of the tax benefit. Otherwise, the child won't know your intent and may hang on to it, assuming it has sentimental value.

Money is like love: The more you give away, the more comes back. When money flows in for you, it's time to help others. Help your children and grandchildren today by transferring some of your appreciated assets and lessening your tax burden. After all, money is meant to be shared. What better way than with your loved ones!

It Costs Nothing but Creates Much

It costs nothing but creates much.

It enriches those who receive without impoverishing those who give.

It happens in a flash, and the memory of it sometimes lasts forever.

None are so rich they can get away without it, and none so poor but are richer for its benefits.

It creates happiness in the home, fosters goodwill in a business, and is the countersign of friends.

It is rest to the weary, daylight to the discouraged, sunshine to the sad, and nature's best antidote for trouble.

Yet it cannot be bought, begged, borrowed or stolen, for it is something that is no earthly good to anyone unless it is given.

And if in the course of the day some of your friends should be too tired to give you one of theirs, why don't you give them one of yours? For nobody needs one so much as those who have none left to give.

A Smile.

There are two kinds of gratitude:
The sudden kind we feel for what we take;
the larger kind we feel for what we give.
—Edwin A. Robinson

We close with this piece that came to us from a close friend over the Internet. We have no clue who the author is but would love to know.

How Do You Live Your Dash?

I read of a man who stood to speak at the funeral of a friend.

He referred to the dates on her tombstone from the beginning to the end.

He noted that first came her date of birth and spoke the following date with tears,

But he said what mattered most of all was the dash between those
   years. (1934–1998)
For that dash represents all the time that she spent alive on earth,
And now only those who loved her know what that little line
   was worth.
For it matters not how much we own—the cars, the house, the cash.
What matters is how we live and love and how we spend our dash.
So think about this long and hard. Are there things you'd like
   to change?
For you never know how much time is left that can still be rearranged.
If we could just slow down enough to consider what's true and real
And always try to understand the way other people feel,
And be less quick to anger and show appreciation more,
And love the people in our lives like we've never loved them before.
If we treat each other with respect and more often wear a smile,
Remembering that this special dash might only last a little while.
So when your eulogy's being read with your life's actions to rehash,
Would you be proud of the things they say and how you spent
   your dash?

5

Invest Wisely

*I want to be in businesses so good that even
a dummy can make money.*
                                    —WARREN BUFFETT

What do you and your family know about investing? By the
end of this book you'll have learned enough to plan a secure
financial future and be worry-free in handling personal and
family money. For now, have some fun and take this pop quiz on sound
investing.

1. The goal in managing your money is to
   a. spend some and save some for the future
   b. keep opportunities high and negative consequences low
   c. hire a broker to handle your finances
   d. take no chances on risky investments

2. Which is the safest investment?
   a. low-risk stocks
   b. U.S. Treasury bonds
   c. a savings account
   d. a money-market checking account

3. Which of the following provides the highest overall return?
   a. real estate
   b. quality stocks with rising dividends
   c. a certificate of deposit
   d. a 401(k) account

4. Which best describes the stock market to you?
   a. high risk and potential loss
   b. a place where it takes money to make money
   c. a place where you can make money if you know what's most important
   d. a place that is only for the rich

5. Why might the public shy away from the stock market?
   a. the unpredictability of the market in the short term
   b. negative headlines and media horror stories
   c. fear of losing money
   d. all the above

6. Roughly how much money do you need to start investing in stocks?
   a. $30
   b. $300
   c. $3000
   d. $30,000

7. What is a common stock?
   a. a company benefit for employees
   b. the company stock most commonly purchased
   c. a stock certificate representing partial ownership of a company
   d. a stock most popular on the Dow-Jones list

8. What is the Dow Jones?
   a. Dow means "able to make money."
   b. Mr. Dow and Mr. Jones were the founders of the industrial average.
   c. the cash dividends of stock.
   d. none of the above.

9. The best way to track stock investments is to
   a. read daily stock market reports
   b. subscribe to several financial magazines
   c. buy shares in the finest companies and watch them grow
   d. listen to the news and financial talk shows

10. What does investing mean?
    a. commiting for a long period with thought of future benefit
    b. buying low-priced stock to produce a quick buck
    c. trying to make the most money in the least amount of time
    d. staying on a budget and not spending more than you make

11. Why should anyone invest?
    a. for a comfortable retirement
    b. for a child's future education
    c. to accomplish financial dreams
    d. all the above

12. The best investment to stay ahead of inflation is
    a. a stock portfolio
    b. a money-market account
    c. certificates of deposit (CDs)
    d. silver or gold

13. What is compound interest?
    a. interest paid from your savings account
    b. interest paid annually instead of monthly
    c. an above-average interest rate paid quarterly
    d. reinvested interest paid systematically

14. If you begin an IRA at 10 percent compound annual interest and contribute $2000 a year, how much will you have after 40 years, based on history?
    a. $80,000
    b. $80,800
    c. $126,000
    d. more than $1 million

15. When it comes to investing your money you should
    a. seek a financial adviser
    b. consult with a trustworthy stockbroker
    c. learn all you can and manage your money wisely
    d. hide it under the mattress

16. How would you describe a high-risk stock?
    a. high probability of losing money
    b. stock in a new hot company
    c. one where you take a chance on its doing well
    d. on the verge of bankruptcy

17. How are stock prices quoted?
    a. according to company profits
    b. The New York Stock Exchange decides on a fair price
    c. The economy and rate of inflation dictate price
    d. in decimal points

18. If a stock in a good company is purchased today at a "fair" price, do you think you'll have a profit in five years?
    a. not sure
    b. depends on the economy
    c. will stay about the same
    d. most likely will make a profit

19. What are some of the "don'ts" of investing?
    a. Do not be fearful, impatient, or greedy.
    b. Do not buy diversified stocks.
    c. Do not ever lend money to someone without interest.
    d. Do not buy high-quality stocks as they are overpriced

20. The most efficient way to invest is to
    a. spread your money across several different markets
    b. invest in a program that is simple, uncomplicated, fun, and profitable
    c. open a portfolio with a broker you were referred to
    d. put your money into a high-interest CD

21. What is a blue-chip stock?
    a. a stock that's in the hot-tip section of the *Wall Street Journal*
    b. a high-risk stock that should be avoided
    c. a stock with a history of doing well
    d. a common stock being purchased most within the last 24 hours

22. What are three good reasons to sell your stock?
    a. stocks are high, great profits, shares about to split
    b. economy is bad, threat of inflation, threat of market collapse
    c. for a tax write-off, to upgrade your portfolio, you need emergency cash
    d. to purchase a home, a vacation, a new car

23. What's the best way to find a full-service broker?
    a. make inquiries of successful investor friends
    b. visit several brokers, and tell them what you want and expect
    c. make sure you know their track records and feel at ease
    d. all of the above

24. Which of the following is most accurate?
    a. The value of a company changes from day to day within the market.
    b. Daily fluctuations in stock prices do not affect the long-term value of a good company.
    c. If you buy more stock in a company, the value increases.
    d. The revenue, earnings, and dividends of a company do not affect its value.

Answers to Investing Quiz:

1. b	5. d	9. c	13. d	17. d	21.c
2. b	6. b	10. a	14. d	18. d	22. c or d
3. b	7.c	11.d	15. c	19. a	23. d
4. c	8. b	12. a	16. c	20. b	24. b

THOU SHALT NOT COMMIT
THE FIVE DEADLY SINS OF INVESTING

*Wisdom consists not so much in knowing what to do
in the ultimate as knowing what to do next.*
—Herbert Hoover

BANK ON IT

IF A MAN HAS MONEY IT'S USUALLY A SIGN THAT HE
KNOWS HOW TO TAKE CARE OF IT.

Thomas Jefferson

We can alter Herbert Hoover's wise counsel to say, "In investing, knowing what not to do may be as important as, if not more important than, knowing what to do."

Any one of the five sins below by itself is potentially dangerous to your and your family's investment health. Together they are lethal. If you are guilty of all five, as an investor you might as well be dead. Your performance surely is, at least so far. Let's go through them to see why they are so harmful to financial success. Then we'll talk about what you and your family should do as investors.

1. Impatience
   You want to make a lot of money in a hurry. (Who doesn't?)
   You buy the latest stock tip you just got from your brother-in-law.
   You won't invest any money in stocks unless you know they'll
   go up right away.

2. Greed
   You want to earn as much money as you can and, because
   you're impatient, in the shortest length of time.
   You're not sure how much money is enough, but you know you
   always want more. Earning 10 to 13 percent in the stock market
   year after year isn't nearly good enough.

3. Fear and Emotion
   You lost a lot of money in 1998–1999. And just when you
   thought you had the market figured out, along came 2000, followed by 2001, 2002, and 2003. You lost a bundle more. You're
   now more afraid of stocks than ever.

A "hot" newsletter advertises that it had the best performance over the last year and recommends 19 stocks that will double in the next year. You can't wait to subscribe for fear of missing out on some easy money in the big recovery that's sure to come. You've never invested in stocks before but have read how horrible things were in the last few years. Your friends claim they always make money in real estate, which is "safe." You'll avoid stocks at all costs and look into real estate and other options.

4. Underdiversification
   Your great-grandfather left your grandfather stock in a railroad because that was where he worked. Your grandfather worked there too. When he died, he left the stock to your father. You father won't sell any shares because he'd have to pay capital gains taxes even though they represent 89 percent of his portfolio and have performed poorly for years.
   You've just put your first $5000 into a mutual fund because "they" manage a diversified portfolio with hundreds of stocks. You, though, own only one security: the mutual fund.

5. Buying low quality
   You have five different stockbrokers or advisers (please choose one) who call you with one idea after another. You buy 100 shares of each and now own 37 different companies even though you don't know much about 32 of them.
   You know for certain that nobody ever got rich buying stodgy high-quality dividend-paying companies. It's growth, not dividends, that matters, because you're in a high income-tax bracket.

Do any of these examples ring true? Some should. They are familiar because people commit the same investing sins over and over and cannot seem to figure out why their performance isn't good. We should know: We've committed them all at one time or another.

You don't have to be impatient because stocks outperform all other investments given enough time, typically 10 years or more. There have been no losing eight-year periods (with dividends reinvested) for more

In the big book of things people more often do wrong than right, investing must certainly top the list, followed closely by wallpapering and eating artichokes.

THE MONEY BOOK OF MONEY, 1987

than 75 years in the Standard & Poor's (S&P 500), an index that represents roughly 80 percent of the value of all U.S. stocks. Edwin LeFevre, a stock millionaire, penned his classic personal story in 1923, *Reminiscences of a Stock Operator*. Regarding the benefits of being patient, he remarked, "It was never my thinking that made the big money for me. It was always sitting. Got that? My sitting tight!"

You don't have to be greedy. A little money set aside regularly for shares of quality companies will grow into a small fortune, if not a large one, over your investment lifetime.

You don't have to be emotional and let things like the tragedy of September 11, 2001, upset your strategy. Forget about day-to-day gyrations in stock prices. They have always been, are, and will continue to be. History proves that the long-term direction of the stock market is one way, and that way is *up*.

You don't have to be fearful of stocks or worry that you can't make profits. Why? Because not committing the five deadly sins listed above almost guarantees that you'll make money, lots of it.

You never have to be underdiversified. As few as eight stocks gives the average investor all the diversity necessary as long as they are (1) high-quality and (2) in different businesses.

Financial calculators abound in numerous websites. One that is worth checking out is www.interest.com/hugh/calc, which offers a wide variety of easy-to-use calculators for uses ranging from retirement plans to mortgages.

You never have to buy low-quality companies if you stick with our exclusive universe of U.S. companies labeled *America's Finest Companies®*.

HOW TO BECOME A MULTIMILLIONAIRE ON JUST $50 A MONTH
(and Spend about One Hour a Year Doing It)

Several years ago we read a newspaper story about Theodore Johnson, who never earned more than $14,000 a year from his job. He squirreled away every extra dollar possible, invested all his money in equities (stocks), and his money greatly multiplied. At the time of the article Johnson was worth more than $70 million. He proved that small amounts of money wisely put to work for the future can grow and multiply rapidly. The same is true for you and your family.

We want everyone, especially young people, to know what we didn't know when we were 18:

- We didn't know what investing was or how to do it.
- We didn't know we could become rich on as little as $50 a month.
- We didn't know that if we started with, and stuck to, a simple investing plan, we'd have more money than we'd ever want or need.

By saving just some of the money you waste ($50 a month and more), you can easily accumulate $600 or more a year. That's more than enough to begin and maintain our powerful program to double your money safely every five to six years (based on history).

How would you like to own some of the finest, most profitable businesses in America, companies such as Coca-Cola, General Electric, Wal-Mart Stores, Hershey's, PepsiCo, and Procter & Gamble? It would be great fun and financially rewarding too, wouldn't it? The only problem is that you don't have the billions of dollars it would take to buy even one of them outright.

But you and your children of any age can easily and simply take advantage of the next best thing by becoming part owners of some of the finest companies in the world, a few dollars at the time. How do you do that? By buying shares and fractions of shares of those companies' stock, in many cases directly from the companies without ever having to go through a stockbroker.

Thanks to the miracle of compound interest, a young shareowner embarking on our investment program of $50 per month at age 18 will accumulate between $879,047 and $1,624,949 by age 60, based on historical stock-market returns. That's only $25,200 in actual dollars invested throughout a 42-year period, yet even that small amount can make anyone a millionaire. You can make your money grow dramatically too no matter what your age is.

Buying and owning shares of stock in the most successful, profitable companies is the fastest, surest way we know to build wealth with almost zero risk. Because we all are customers of many of these top-notch companies, we're already making them rich. Now we'll allow them to help us get rich too.

Let's be specific. You can go to McDonald's for a meal, drink Coca-Cola or Pepsi, brush your teeth with toothpaste from Colgate-Palmolive or Procter & Gamble, light your home and office with products from General Electric, buy home renovation supplies at Home Depot or Lowe's, and on the way home pick up a few things from Walgreens. Not only would you make money by investing in companies such as these, you also would contribute to their bottom lines, thus enhancing their profits. And because you are an owner, that would boost your bottom line too.

These companies and more than 300 others like them are in the select universe we recommend exclusively for investing. To qualify for our trademarked group known as *America's Finest Companies*® (this information is published annually), corporations must be U.S.-based and have a minimum of 10 consecutive years of increases in earnings or dividends. Out of more than 19,000 publicly traded companies, fewer than 2 percent make it! These are the thoroughbreds of American industry from which you will select your portfolio.

A BRIEF HISTORY OF THE STOCK MARKET

Before we go any further, let us share with you a brief stock-market history that not only explains how stocks work but also shows how substantial riches can be accumulated.

By the time Columbus set sail for what he thought were the East Indies (he landed in the Caribbean instead), shares of various commodities and what were then called joint-stock companies were actively bought and sold in Antwerp, Belgium. The city of Antwerp claims that among the world's more than 170 stock exchanges, its exchange is the oldest, having been founded in 1531. Amsterdam lays claim to the second oldest with a start-up date of 1602.

Stock certificates of ownership were sold to investors in some European countries to finance powerhouse enterprises such as the United East India Company, which came to life in 1602. That company returned about 18 percent annually to investors for three decades ($1 grew to more than $143), an incredible performance, and remained in business until 1799.

Stock trading on a limited basis existed well before Jesus was born. The early Romans formed joint-stock companies and sold pieces of them to the public. The word *company* comes from the Latin *cum* ("with") and *panis* ("bread") because business in those days often was conducted over a meal just as it so frequently is today. Under the law, joint-stock companies of that time could do just two things: government contracting and tax collecting. What fantastic businesses to invest in! Capital (money) was raised by selling *partes* ("shares") to willing investors.

Securities markets in the United States can be traced back to the late 1700s. In 1789 Congress authorized and issued $80 million of government bonds to pay down war debts and inject money into the fledgling country's economy, thus creating the first "money market." According to *American Heritage* magazine, "The new United States was desperately short of money in any reliable or secured form. Accounts were still kept in pounds, shillings, and pence."

Brokers (they were called stockjobbers) traded stocks and bonds literally in the street. The word *broker* was derived from wine merchants, who broached (tapped) their wine kegs. *Broacher* later was shortened to *broker*. Brokers bought and sold primarily government bonds as well as stocks offered by the infant Bank of the United States. When the weather turned sour, they retreated to coffeehouses (presumably to warm up) to carry on their business.

The several dozen established brokers in New York City operated a highly risky "market." James Madison was so concerned, he fired off a letter to Thomas Jefferson warning that "stock jobbing drowns every other subject. The coffeehouse is an eternal buzz with the gamblers." Since stock brokering, trading, or whatever you want to call it was so risky in the early days, the eighteenth-century phrase "gambling in the stock market" still has deep meaning for many Americans.

In 1792, 24 brokers and merchants gathered at Corre's Hotel to sign the Buttonwood Agreement, which was written on the front and back on a sheet of paper: "We, the Subscribers, Brokers for the Purchase and Sale of Public Stocks, do hereby solemnly pledge ourselves to each other that we will not buy or sell, from this day, for any person whatsoever, any kind of Public Stock at a less rate than one-quarter per cent Commission on the Special value, and that we will give preference to each other in our negotiations."

This unusual contract laid the foundation for the later-to-be-formed (in 1817) New York Stock and Exchange Board. The following winter the brokers built a home for themselves, the Tontine Coffee House, on the corner of Water and Wall streets in New York, the nation's capital at that time.

The famous street named Wall, one of the best known in the world, is only four blocks long. It lies on the site of the original wall (stockade) built at the tip of Manhattan Island. In 1644 Dutch settlers laid a brushwood barrier to keep Indians out and cattle in. Nine years later Governor Peter Stuyvesant replaced it with a nine-foot-high palisade.

Wall Street is named for that barrier, not for the high buildings on both sides of the street that currently create walls.

Wall Street is the common name for the American financial institutions, markets, and mechanisms that formalized and democratized the capital-formation (money-raising) process that helps companies thrive. Wall Street, with the New York Stock Exchange (NYSE) as its flagship, has allowed millions of Americans of all ages to participate in this country's unmatched growth through the ownership of common stocks. In its spring 1992 issue dedicated to the Big Board (the NYSE), *Life* magazine observed, "For two centuries, men (and much more recently women) have met at the convergence of Wall and Broad streets in lower Manhattan to buy, sell and haggle, all in the name of capitalism. They have not always done so politely . . . or fairly. But as Americans traded, so the country was built. Canals, Railroads, Automobiles, Electronics. Ideas may spring from laboratories, but the money that turns them into reality is raised here."

With capitalism spreading rapidly across the globe, new stock exchanges have sprouted behind what used to be the Iron Curtain. Poland opened a stock market in early 1991 in the old Communist Party headquarters (ironic, isn't it?). The Polish market was funded by British money and modeled after France's Bourse, another name for a stock exchange or place of meeting to conduct business. Initially, trading (buying and selling) in Poland took place only once a week in five different companies, but it has expanded to include hundreds more. St. Petersburg opened its exchange (the *Wall Street Journal* calls a stock exchange the "icon of capitalism") on the third floor of the former Communist Party headquarters.

WHAT IS A STOCK AND HOW DOES IT WORK?

What exactly is a common stock? It's a security (stock certificate) representing proportionate ownership (an investor's share) of a publicly traded company. There are more than 19,000 public companies in America. You can buy shares in most of them through any stockbroker and directly from hundreds of the companies. These shares are traded (bought and sold) on the New York Stock Exchange, the American Stock Exchange

(ASE), or the NASDAQ over-the-counter (OTC) exchange. They range in price from a penny a share to Berkshire-Hathaway on the NYSE, the highest-priced stock in the world, which has sold for as much as $84,000 for one share.

Where did the words *common stock* come from? Here's our theory. William Bradford, governor of the Plymouth Colony, reported that under an agreement with the Pilgrims' sponsors from England, "all profit" (crops, fish, and trade goods) would "remain still in the common stock." All Pilgrims were allowed to share their food and goods from the common stock, just as all investors can make profits by investing (sharing) in the "common stock" of public companies.

Stocks originally were priced in points instead of dollars. One point equals $1.00. One-half point equals $0.50, one-quarter point $0.25, and one-eighth point $0.125. Stocks traded in eighths rather than tenths (like money). Isn't that strange?

There's a practical reason. When stock trading began in colonial days, coins were in short supply. To make coinage go further, Spanish silver dollars were sliced into halves, then halved and halved again. The result? The dollar could be divided into eight bits. Each bit was one-eighth of a dollar. Together, eight bits "pieces of eight" equal a dollar. Today stocks are traded down to two decimal places.

Here's how stocks work. In this example MakeMoney Enterprises (MME), a fictitious company, has 1 million shares outstanding. Each share sells for 20 (stock prices are quoted without the dollar sign), and so MME's total stock is worth $20 million. If you invest $4000 in MME at its current price, you can purchase 200 shares.

When you purchase your shares, you will own part of the company. Although it's a tiny part (a five thousandth), it's all yours. Now that you are a part owner of MME, what good is it? Let's use this example to find out.

MME earns $2 million after taxes in 2003. Dividing earnings by the number of shares (1 million), each share has $2.00. MME provides money out of earnings, a cash dividend, as an incentive for you to buy and hold its shares. (Not all companies pay dividends, but the bulk of *America's Finest Companies®* do.) Out of the $2.00 per share of earnings, MME pays you half: $1.00. That dollar is your immediate reward for owning a piece of the company.

MME keeps (retains) the other half and plows it back into the business for reasons similar to why humans eat daily to survive. Retained earnings go for research and product development, to build a new plant, to purchase new equipment, to hire more people—to grow.

By keeping the dollar not paid to you, MME is now worth $1.00 more per share for each share outstanding than it was before. The company's total asset value increases $1 million (1 million shares times $1.00 per share retained). MME's business prospers. Five years from now (2008) its earnings have risen 50 percent to $3.00 per share. And as a further reward to you for holding the shares as opposed to selling them, the company boosts its dividend (as it has done every year since you bought your shares) to the newest annual rate of $1.50. Each year it keeps as much as it pays you, and that amount kept annually enhances MME's value.

Your annual income from owning the company is increasing. By 2013 earnings per share are $5.00. Your dividend is now $2.50 per share, up 150 percent over 2003. The company keeps $2.50 per share that year, $2.5 million in total, to further boost asset value by that amount.

Question: If the share price is 20 in 2003 when you buy into MME and the shares are not overpriced, do you think the price will be higher in 2008 than in 2003? Will it be even higher in 2013?

Answer: If the share price maintains the same relationship to its earnings and dividend, it will rise to 30 in 2008 and to 50 by 2013.

Your original investment of 200 shares at 20 each will be worth $10,000 in 2008. Your cost: $4000. Your profit: $6000. Between 2003 and 2013 your annual income from dividends alone in MME will jump from $200 to $500. Your yearly yield on the original investment will rise to 12.5 percent ($500 in dividends divided by the $4000 original cost), a handsome return.

Over a period of years the majority of publicly owned companies grow. (All the companies we recommend are growing.) Growing companies earn more money. They pay out more cash as dividends. They plow back a growing stream of earnings into their businesses, thus enhancing the value of those businesses. This explains why stock prices always go up in the long run. The Dow Jones Industrial Average, the most famous measure of stock prices, rose from 88 in 1912 to more than

11,000 by the end of 1999 before settling back to around 9000 as we went to press. That's from price appreciation alone and excludes cash dividends. With dividends reinvested, the Dow would be well above 100,000.

Having studied and analyzed hundreds of the enterprises in *America's Finest Companies*® over the years, we learned that they share the following winning traits:

1. The finest companies serve customers and employees with a passion.
2. Their managements are strong and decisive.
3. Each company knows where it wants to go.
4. They carve out their own paths for growth.
5. They are creative and innovative.
6. They control expenses carefully.
7. They respond to problems rather than react to them.

We'll add that principles always matter in money matters and in life. Picture this. You're the coach. Your lacrosse team is 13–0 with a few games to go. Then 32 of your 38 players admit that they've violated a pledge not to use alcohol, drugs, or tobacco. You suspend them for four games. Your perfect season is over.

This happened at Charlotte Country Day School, the school our daughter Gracie attended for 13 years. The coach of the team is Brad Touma, who also teaches Junior Achievement's Applied Economics.

Bill is a consultant to Brad's class and has taught investing there for the last 17 years. Touma is a class act by anyone's standards. He sacrificed a great shot at an undefeated season because he knows that principles always matter.

Former *Forbes* columnist John Rutledge wrote an inspiring article several years ago called "Teaching Things That Really Matter." He says that a business should "be built and managed on a foundation of solid principles." He also opines that "there is such an emphasis today on being cool and being a winner that we are forgetting what a valuable teacher losing can be."

Rutledge believes that the three bedrock essentials of business success are (1) understanding that a good reputation is a major form of

A Cardinal Rule in Investing: Don't Buy Just Anything

Here's what can happen when you speculate. It can kill your pocketbook. Case in point, former high-flyer Polaroid (PRD). Back in the early 1970s, a period few investors today remember, PRD was one of the supreme "nifty fifty," a group of stocks it was said one could buy at any price and eventually come out okay if one held on long enough. Had our universe of companies been around at that time, most of the 50 would not have qualified through 10 years of rising earnings or dividends.

Tampax (now Tambrands), Eastman Kodak, Xerox, and International Flavors & Fragrances were all part of that bunch. They and many others like them have long since collapsed. So has Polaroid. Not that long ago, the company laid off 11 percent of its workers and took a $90 million restructuring charge as product demand flagged. One of its biggest problems was the growing popularity of digital photography, which threatened Polaroid's instant film and led the company to introduce devices that can print digital photographs instantly. Now it is almost gone. Although it traded as high as 90 per share more than two decades ago, there is no longer a public market.

capital, (2) distinguishing between people who are trustworthy and those who aren't, and (3) realizing that it's okay to fail as long as you keep trying.

We were on a radio show talking about how to become a millionaire by using time-proven, conservative wealth-building principles. One host, Julie, remarked that her father had just made a killing in a stock we'd never heard of and asked if that was the type of company we recommended buying.

Our answer was no. We believe you should invest only in companies with a track record of success. Doing anything else is speculating. We explained that we buy—and recommend in our newsletter to Staton Institute members that they buy—only the shares of *America's Finest*

Companies®, the top 2.0 percent of all U.S. public companies, the thoroughbreds of American industry.

We know that if corporations including Coca-Cola and McDonald's and Exxon and Colgate-Palmolive and Wm. Wrigley Jr. don't succeed, no other companies will either. But if they continue to grow and prosper as they have through the decades, we—the shareowners—also will grow and prosper. There is no other option.

This simple concept elegantly explains how to become very rich just as Einstein's simple and elegant e $= mc^2$ explains the universe. Why make making a fortune for you and yours so terribly complicated (as the financial community does so well) when it is so easy? That's the beauty of *Worry-Free Family Finances*.

If you invest exclusively in *America's Finest Companies*®, you'll be putting the seven traits listed above to work for you in your portfolio. Assuming that the historical performance of their stocks continues (and there's no reason for it not to), you'll do far better than most professional money managers.

GETTING STARTED AS WORRY-FREE INVESTORS

To get started on your path to becoming a multimillionaire, you first choose five to eight companies to buy from our exclusive list beginning on page 122. Each of these companies pays a quarterly cash dividend to stockholders on each share of stock they own; this is one of a shareowner's rewards for owning part of a company.

Cash dividend checks are mailed to you each quarter and often can be deposited automatically into your bank account. Or if directed by you (which is what we recommend), dividends are reinvested by the company on your behalf to purchase additional shares and fractions of shares through a dividend reinvestment plan (DRP). When you elect to have your dividends reinvested in a DRP rather than paid to you directly, the company uses your money to help it grow. You benefit by increasing the number of shares you own every quarter, year after year. That's why we recommend reinvesting in DRPs. It's a simple, sure, worry-free route to building wealth surely and steadily.

From the end of 1925 through the end of 2002, roughly 94 percent of the total return from stocks (as measured by the broadest-based stock-market index, the S&P 500) came from reinvested dividends. The remaining 6 percent came from rising prices. That is why reinvesting your dividends is critical to accumulating wealth for your family and you.

Stocks have earned (dividends plus price appreciation) some 12 to 13 percent a year since the end of World War II, much more than any other investment has. Specifically, according to *The Value Line Investment Survey*, the annual return from the Dow Jones Industrial Average (the oldest stock-market index, formed in 1894) for the last 50 years (through 2001) was 11.7 percent, 16.5 percent for the last 20, and 14.7 percent for the last 10. Meanwhile, inflation grew at 4.0 percent for the last 50 years, 3.4 percent for the last 20, and 2.7 percent for the last 10. (You can see how well just the average stock has performed vis-à-vis inflation.)

Because our exclusive companies historically outperform the stock market, a portfolio of stocks chosen from this universe should grow faster than that—13 to 15 percent or more annually, or some 10 to 30 percent faster than the typical stock. At that rate, your investments double in value roughly every five to five and a half years. Fifty dollars per month growing at 13 to 15 percent will be worth:

Period	Total Invested	$50 per Month Will Grow to
10 years	$6,000	$ 12,488–$14,010
20 years	$12,000	$ 54,881–$70,686
30 years	$18,000	$198,789–$299,974
40 years	$24,000	$817,717–$1,570,188

IT'S NEVER TOO LATE TO START

If a person waits until age 25 to 30 to begin investing in *America's Finest Companies*®, he or she can still build up to $1 million and more by age 65 to 70 yet never have to invest more than $50 each month, again assuming that long-term stock performance holds up as it has consistently since World War II.

But what if you're older than that? Obviously it will take more money per month, but the task of getting where you need to be financially—

when you want to be there—is not nearly as formidable as you might think. We developed the following table to help you and everyone in your family regardless of age:

For the Newborn Baby: Starting at Age 0

Years Old	20	30	40	50	60
$ per Month					
$50	57,276	221,032	817,717	2,991,876	10,913,934
$100	114,552	442,064	1,635,434	5,983,752	21,827,868
$200	229,552	884,128	3,270,868	11,967,506	43,655,735
$400	458,208	1,768,256	6,541,736	23,935,012	87,311,470
$1000	1,145,519	4,420,646	16,354,339	59,837,529	218,278,675
$2000	2,291,038	8,841,292	32,708,678	119,675,058	436,557,350

For the Young Person: Starting at Age 20

Years Old	30	40	50	60	70
$ per Month					
$50	12,334	57,276	221,032	817,717	2,991,876
$100	24,668	114,552	442,064	1,635,434	5,983,752
$200	49,336	229,104	884,128	3,270,868	11,967,506
$400	98,672	458,208	1,768,256	6,541,736	23,935,012
$1000	246,681	1,145,519	4,420,646	16,354,339	59,837,529
$2000	493,363	2,291,038	8,841,292	32,708,678	119,675,058

For the Baby Boomer: Starting at Age 40

Years Old	50	60	70	80
$ per Month				
$50	12,334	57,276	221,032	817,717
$100	24,668	114,552	442,064	1,635,434
$200	49,336	229,104	884,128	3,270,868
$400	98,672	458,208	1,768,256	6,541,736
$1000	246,681	1,145,519	4,420,646	16,354,339

These projections assume a 13 percent annual return, the historical rate of growth for the stock market for the last five decades. There is no guarantee that our universe of stocks or any stocks will earn such returns in the future.

We encourage parents and grandparents to begin the $50 a month multimillionaire investment program for their children and grandchildren as early as possible. Fifty dollars per month (beginning at birth) earning 13 percent annually grows to $43,161 by the time a child turns 19. If *no more* contributions are made and the money continues growing at 13 percent (taxes excluded), it will be worth

$2.2 million at age 50
$7.3 million at age 60
$24.8 million at age 70

If the portfolio earns 15 percent and doubles every five years, the numbers are

$4.8 million by age 50
$19.6 million by age 60
$79.1 million by age 70

By starting early enough, you and everyone in your family can become multimillionaires on as little as $50 a month or perhaps even less. Where else can you get that kind of return from such a small amount of money, plus have so much fun doing it?

Step 1: Choose Five to Eight of *America's Finest Companies* to Buy

To begin your investment program, choose at least five of the companies from the following list and buy one or more shares of each (see step 2 for details on how to buy). At this date each company requires only one share to participate in its dividend reinvestment plan. Many charge no commissions or service fees, and so 100 percent of your investment money goes to work for you. On occasion a company may change its requirements, so before investing in any of the companies it's best to call, write, or log on to a company's website. Shown below are all of *America's Finest Companies*® with a minimum 15 straight years of higher dividends per share and dividend reinvestment plans. We also show the minimum direct investment if the company has one, the phone number, and the website.

Company	Symbol	Industry	DRP	Minimum	Years	Phone	Website
3M Co.	MMM	Manufacturing	X		44	651-733-8206	3m
Abbott Laboratories	ABT	Health care	X		30	847-937-7300	abbott
AFLAC Inc.	AFL	Insurance, life	X	1000	20	800-235-2667	aflac
Air Products & Chemicals	APD	Chemicals	X	500	20	800-247-6525	airproducts
ALLTEL Corp.	AT	Telephone	X		42	877-446-3628	alltel
American States Water	AW	Water utility	X	500	50	909-394-3600	aswater
AmSouth Bancorporation	ASO	Banking	X		30	205-801-0265	amsouth
Anheuser-Busch Cos. Inc.	BUD	Alcoholic beverages	X		28	800-342-5283	anheuser-busch
Associated Banc-Corp.	ASBC	Banking	X		32	800-236-2722	associatedbank
Avery Dennison Corp.	AVY	Manufacturing	X	500	27	626-304-2000	averydennison
BancorpSouth Inc.	BXS	Banking	X		20	601-680-2000	bancorpsouth
Bandag Inc.	BDG	Auto parts	X		26	319-262-1400	bandag
Bank of America Corp.	BAC	Banking	X	1000	25	800-521-3984	bankofamerica
Banta Corp.	BN	Printing	X		25	920-751-7777	banta
Bard, C.R. Inc.	BCR	Medical products	X	250	31	908-277-8000	crbard
BB&T Corp.	BBT	Banking	X		21	336-733-3058	bbandt
Becton, Dickinson & Co.	BDX	Medical products	X	250	31	800-284-6845	bd
Bemis Co.	BMS	Containers	X		19	612-376-3030	bemis
Black Hills Corp.	BKH	Electric utility	X		32	605-721-1700	blackhillscorp
Brown-Forman Corp.	BF.B	Alcoholic beverages	X		18	502-585-1100	brown-forman
California Water Service Group	CWT	Water utility	X	500	35	800-750-8200	calwater

Company	Symbol	Industry	DRP	Minimum	Years	Phone	Website
Carlisle Companies Inc.	CSL	Manufacturing	X		26	315-474-2500	carlisle
CenturyTel Inc.	CTL	Telephone	X		29	800-833-1188	centurytel
Chubb Corp.	CB	Insurance, property	X		38	908-903-2000	chubb
Cincinnati Financial Corp.	CINF	Insurance, property	X		42	513-870-2639	cinfin
Citizens Banking Corp.	CBCF	Banking	X		19	810-257-2593	cbclientsfirst
CLARCOR Inc.	CLC	Machinery	X		19	815-962-8867	clarcor
Cleco Corp.	CNL	Electric utility	X		31	800-253-2652	cleco
Clorox Co.	CLX	Household products.	X		24	510-271-2927	clorox
Coca-Cola Co.	KO	Soft drink	X		40	888-265-3747	coca-cola
Colgate-Palmolive Co.	CL	Household products	X		40	800-850-2654	colgate-palmolive
Comerica Inc.	CMA	Banking	X		59	800-521-1190	comerica
Compass Bancshares Inc.	CBSS	Banking	X		21	205-297-6750	compassweb
ConAgra Foods Inc.	CAG	Foods	X		27	402-595-4000	conagra
Connecticut Water Service	CTWS	Water utility	X	100	33	800-428-3985	ctwater
Diebold Inc.	DBD	Office equipment and supplies	X	500	49	800-766-5859	diebold
Donnelley, R.R & Sons Co.	DNY	Printing	X		31	312-326-8018	rrdonnelley
Emerson Co.	EMR	Electrical equipment	X		46	314-553-2197	emersonelectric
Energen Corp.	EGN	Natural gas	X	250	20	800-654-3206	energen
Exxon Mobil Corp.	XOM	Oil	X	250	20	972-444-1156	exxonmobil
Fannie Mae	FNM	Financial	X	250	17	800-366-2968	fanniemae
Federal Realty Inv. Trust	FRT	Real estate investment trust	X		35	800-658-8980	federalrealty
First Tennessee National	FTN	Banking	X		25	800-410-4577	firsttennessee
First Virginia Banks Inc.	FVB	Banking	X		26	800-995-9416	firstvirginia

Company	Symbol	Industry	DRP	Minimum	Years	Phone	Website
FirstMerit Corp.	FMER	Banking	X		21	330-996-6300	FirstMerit
Fuller, H.B. Co.	FULL	Chemicals	X		34	800-214-2523	hbfuller
Gannett Co. Inc.	GCI	Publishing	X		32	703-284-6960	gannett
GATX Corp.	GMT	Transportation	X		17	800-428-8161	gatx
General Electric Co.	GE	Electrical equipment	X	250	27	800-786-2543	ge
Genuine Parts Co.	GPC	Auto parts	X		46	770-953-1700	genpt
Gorman-Rupp Co.	GRC(A)	Manufacturing	X		30	419-755-1294	gormanrupp
Hillenbrand Industries Inc.	HB	Manufacturing	X	250	30	812-934-8400	hillenbrand
Hormel Foods Corp.	HRL	Foods	X		36	507-437-5669	hormel
Illinois Tool Works Inc.	ITW	Manufacturing	X		40	847-657-4104	itw
Jefferson-Pilot Corp.	JP	Insurance, life	X		34	336-691-3379	jpfinancial
Johnson & Johnson	JNJ	Health care	X		40	800-950-5089	jnj
Johnson Controls Inc.	JCI	Manufacturing	X	50	27	414-524-2363	johnsoncontrols
KeyCorp	KEY	Banking	X		22	216-689-4221	key
Kimberly-Clark Corp.	KMB	Household products	X		30	800-639-1352	kimberly-clark
Lancaster Colony Corp.	LANC	Foods	X		40	614-224-7141	lancastercolony
La-Z-Boy Inc.	LZB	Household furniture	X		22	734-241-4414	la-z-boy
Lilly, Eli & Co.	LLY	Health care	X	1000	35	800-833-8699	lilly
Lincoln National Corp.	LNC	Insurance, life	X	2000	19	800-237-2920	lnc
Lowe's Companies Inc.	LOW	Retail	X	250	22	336-658-5239	lowes
M&T Bank Corp.	MTB	Banking	X		22	716-842-5445	mandtbank
Madison Gas & Electric Co.	MGEE	Electric utility	X	50	22	800-356-6423	mge

Company	Symbol	Industry	DRP	Minimum	Years	Phone	Website
Marshall & Ilsley Corp.	MI	Banking	X		30	800-318-0208	micorp
May Department Stores Co.	MAY	Retail	X		28	314-342-6300	maycompany
Medtronic Inc.	MDT	Medical products	X		25	612-574-3035	medtronic
Mercantile Bankshares Corp.	MRBK	Banking	X		26	410-347-8039	mrbk
Merck & Co. Inc.	MRK	Health care	X	350	27	908-423-5881	merck
Modine Manufacturing Co.	MODI	Auto parts	X	500	19	800-813-3324	info@modine
National Commerce Bancorp.	NCBC	Banking	X		28	901-523-3434	ncbcorp
National Fuel Gas Co.	NFG	Natural gas	X	1000	31	716-857-6987	nationalfuelgas
Nordson Corp.	NDSN	Machinery	X		39	440-414-5344	nordson
Nucor Corp.	NUE	Steel	X		30	704-366-7000	nucor
NW Natural	NWN	Natural gas	X		47	800-422-4012	nwnatural
Otter Tail Corp.	OTTR	Electric utility	X		27	800-664-1259	ottertail
Pacific Century Financial	BOH	Banking	X	250	24	808-537-8037	boh
Pentair Inc.	PNR	Manufacturing	X		26	651-636-7920	pentair
Peoples Energy Corp.	PGL	Natural gas	X	250	19	800-228-6888	peoplesenergy
Pfizer Inc.	PFE	Health care	X	500	35	212-573-2668	pfizer
Philip Morris Cos. Inc.	MO	Tobacco	X		37	800-367-5415	philipmorris
Piedmont Nat. Gas Co.	PNY	Natural gas	X	250	24	704-364-3483	piedmontng
Pitney Bowes Inc.	PBI	Office equipment and supplies	X		20	203-356-5000	pitneybowes
Procter & Gamble Co.	PG	Household products	X	250	47	800-742-6253	pg.com/investor
Quaker Chemical Corp.	KWR	Chemicals	X		31	610-832-4119	quakerchem

Company	Symbol	Industry	DRP	Minimum	Years	Phone	Website
Questar Corp.	STR	Natural gas	X	250	25	801-324-5000	questar
Regions Financial Corp.	RGBK	Banking	X	1000	31	800-922-3468	regionsbank
RLI Corp.	RLI	Insurance, property	X		26	800-331-4929	rlicorp
RPM Inc.	RPM	Chemicals	X		29	800-776-4488	rpminc
Sara Lee Corp.	SLE	Foods	X		26	888-422-9881	saralee
SBC Communications Inc.	SBC	Telephone	X	500	17	800-351-7221	sbc
Schering-Plough Corp.	SGP	Health care	X		17	973-822-7000	schering-plough
SEMCO Energy Corp.	SEN	Natural gas	X	250	26	800-225-7647	semcoenergy
ServiceMaster Co.	SVM	Special services	X		32	630-271-1300	servicemaster
Sherwin-Williams Co.	SHW	Building materials	X		23	216-566-2000	sherwin-williams
Sonoco Products Co.	SON	Containers	X	250	20	843-383-7635	sonoco
SouthTrust Corp.	SOTR	Banking	X		33	205-254-6868	southtrust
St. Paul Companies	SPC	Insurance, property	X		17	651-310-7911	stpaul
Stanley Works	SWK	Hardware and tools	X		35	860-827-3833	stanleyworks
SunTrust Banks Inc.	STI	Banking	X		27	404-588-7711	suntrust
SUPERVALU INC.	SVU	Distributor	X		31	612-828-4599	supervalu
Susquehanna Bancshares	SUSQ	Banking	X	250	20	717-625-6305	susqbanc
SYSCO Corp.	SYY	Distributor	X		32	800-337-9726	sysco
Target Corp.	TGT	Retail	X	500	29	612-761-6736	target
Tennant Co.	TNC	Machinery	X		31	763-540-1553	tennantco
Tompkins Trustco Inc.	TMP(A)	Banking	X	100	20	607-273-3210	tompkinstrustco
U.S. Bancorp Inc.	USB	Banking	X		45	612-973-2264	usbank

126

Company	Symbol	Industry	DRP	Minimum	Years	Phone	Website
United Dominion Realty Trust	UDR	Real estate investment trust	X		27	804-780-2691	udrt
Universal Corp.	UVV	Tobacco	X		32	804-254-8689	universalcorp
VF Corp.	VFC	Textile/apparel	X		30	336-547-6000	vfc
Walgreen Co.	WAG	Retail drug	X	50	26	847-914-2972	walgreens
Wal-Mart Stores Inc.	WMT	Retail	X	250	19	501-273-4000	wal-mart
Washington REIT	WRE	Real estate investment trust	X	250	33	800-565-9748	writ
Weingarten Realty Investors	WRI	Real estate investment trust	X	500	18	800-298-9974	weingarten
WesBanco Inc.	WSBC	Banking	X		17	304-234-9000	wesbanco
WGL Holdings Inc.	WGL	Natural gas	X		26	800-221-9427	wglholdings
Wilmington Trust Corp.	WL	Banking	X		21	800-441-7120	wilmingtontrust
WPS Resources Corp.	WPS	Electric utility	X	100	44	800-236-1551	wpsr
Wrigley, Wm. Jr. Co.	WWY	Foods	X		22	800-874-0474	wrigley

If you call, tell the operator you want information about the company's DRP. You'll be transferred to investor/shareholder relations, or you might be given a toll-free number. When you get where you need to be, tell the person you want to be in the company's DRP and need to be assured that it takes only one share to begin (of course you can start with more shares if you can afford it). If you call five companies, it should take no more than an hour, if that long. Ask each company you contact to mail you a DRP packet.

You can begin by investing with just one company, but ultimately you'll want to own at least five companies (eight is even better) for proper diversity, each in a different industry.

Step Two: Purchase Your First Shares

In 1994, just after we were married, we helped Mary's two children's get started on this program. We gave Tate and Whitney $2500 apiece, and they bought one share each of General Electric, First Union Corp. (now Wachovia Corp.), McGraw-Hill, Coca-Cola, and Colgate-Palmolive. By the end of 2000 each portfolio was worth more than $8000.

To begin, we used our stockbroker to purchase one share of each company for each child. (The rest of the money was put to work as we describe in step 3.) The five shares cost $235.64, plus $68.71 in commissions for the broker. (Depending on where you buy your initial shares, the commissions may be more or less than that.) The total was $304.35 per child. It took about 10 minutes to open the accounts, which is about the same amount of time it will take you.

We asked that the shares be registered in Tate and Whitney's names and mailed to our home address.

Please don't let the thought of opening a brokerage account intimidate you. All it takes is a few minutes on the phone for the broker (they're listed in the Yellow Pages under "Stock and Bond Brokers") to get some basic (nothing private) information. Then there'll be one or two pieces of paper to sign, and that's it. Done. Any broker can handle this simple transaction quickly and easily for you. A smart broker will be helpful and make you feel comfortable with what you're doing. If you don't feel that way, hang up and call another one.

Based on our extensive research, these are some of the most consumer-friendly online discount brokers. We advise you to check them all.

Muriel Siebert	siebertnet.com
TD Waterhouse	tdwaterhouse.com
HarrisDirect	harrisdirect.com
Charles Schwab	schwab.com
Quick & Reilly	quickandreilly.com

In addition, your bank could be a good place to start. More and more banks offer discount-brokerage services, including online investing, and are especially happy to help their customers. If your bank doesn't have a brokerage arm, another bank in your community will.

For additional information about how to buy shares of *America's Finest Companies®* in small-dollar amounts, please thoroughly check out these excellent websites: www.sharebuilder.com, www.netstockdirect.com, and www.oneshare.com. The list of companies above also includes websites. If the company lets you purchase shares directly from the company without going through a broker (as Home Depot does), that is indicated, along with the amount of money required for the initial investment. Most companies require at least $100 to get started, and so if your budget won't allow for that amount, buying direct may prove too expensive. Otherwise, it's the simplest way to invest in specific companies and avoid stockbrokers altogether.

Here are a few examples. Walgreen (stock symbol WAG, 888-368-7346) offers a direct-purchase plan in which any investor can purchase the stock without going through a stockbroker. Minimum starting investment: $50. This company, like so many others, will set up regular investing through electronic monthly debits from your checking or savings account with a one-time enrollment fee of only $10. To add to your investments by check, the fee is $5 plus 10 cents a share, far cheaper than doing it through any broker we know of. If you use a debit card, the fee drops to $1.50 per transaction and 10 cents per share.

One of the great innovations for do-it-yourself investors is online direct investing, and companies such as General Electric are leading the way. On their special website you can see your account balance and current transaction/disbursement check history, with the ability to not only buy shares online but also sell them online, with small fees to buy or sell. For more information, visit www.ge.com/investor or phone 800-STOCK-GE.

In our wealth-building program you can buy one share of company A, then save more money and buy a share of company B, and so forth. But we don't recommend that because it's too cumbersome. Regardless of the amount you're saving each month ($15, $25, $50, $100), wait until you have enough set aside to buy one share each of at least five different companies. Making all the purchases at once will be less of a hassle, especially when you are going through a broker.

Once you open your account and make your purchases, you'll get a confirmation slip for each company similar to the one shown below. It shows the name, address, and phone number of the broker. It also shows the name and address of the purchaser, but in this example that's been deleted. The purchase was made on August 19, 1994, for 26 5/8 ($26.63). The commission was $9.48 ($5.48 plus $4.00) for a total of $36.11.

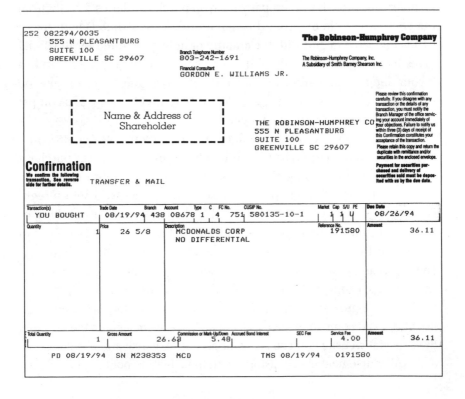

You must send a check immediately to pay for the stock because you're not allowed by law to wait until the end of the month as you can do with other bills. The broker is required to have the money in hand on the third business day after your purchase.

Once you receive your purchase confirmations, be sure to put them in a safe place. You'll need them for tax purposes if you ever decide to sell your original shares, which you most likely won't do.

Some brokers charge a minimum transaction fee for small (including one-share) purchases. This fee can be as high as $40 to $50 for each of the individual shares you buy but should not be more than that. The good news is that you'll buy future shares directly from the companies and will not have to pay the broker ever again.

Step 3: Sign Up for Dividend Reinvestment

Ask your broker to register the shares in the name of the owner (you or your child or grandchild) and mail the shares to you. You must do this so that you can take advantage of the power of dividend reinvestment plans. You will receive a stock certificate like the one shown below for every stock purchased. They usually come within three weeks. Put these

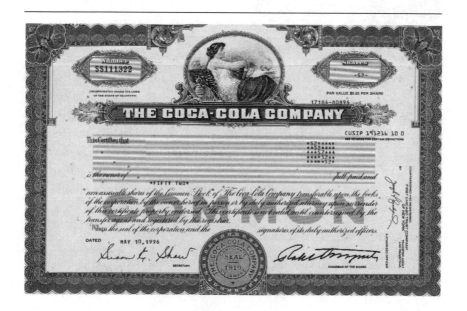

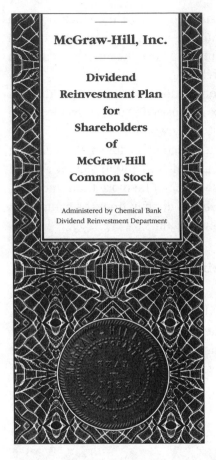

McGraw-Hill, Inc.

Dividend
Reinvestment Plan
for
Shareholders
of
McGraw-Hill
Common Stock

Administered by Chemical Bank
Dividend Reinvestment Department

certificate(s) in a safe place or, for kids, frame and hang them on their walls. Many are colorful and some are not, but that's not the point. They remind youth of what they own.

You'll receive sign-up forms for the DRPs after the stock certificates come, or they may be included with the first dividend check. But there's no need to wait that long. Remember that in step 1 we recommended that before investing you should ask each company you contact to mail you a dividend reinvestment plan packet. If you do that, you'll already have the DRP sign-up forms. Once you've bought shares, fill in your name on the DRP forms exactly as it appears on the confirmations from your broker and mail them back in the postage-paid envelopes. In most cases, that's not even necessary because the forms come preprinted.

A booklet similar to the one shown giving the specifics of the plan also will be enclosed in the DRP packet, and there's usually a toll-free number with the website included in case you have a question.

Almost all companies that pay dividends pay once per quarter (the rest pay annually like McDonald's). After you've signed on for a company's DRP, the next time a dividend is paid, it will be used to buy whole and fractional shares of stock instead of being sent to you.

Step 4: Buy More Shares for Free

Every quarter you'll receive a dividend reinvestment statement from each of your companies showing how many shares or parts of shares were bought and at what price. The companies in whose DRPs you are participating hold the shares. You don't have to keep track of them. At or near the end of every calendar year (after the fourth quarterly dividend has been reinvested), you'll get a final DRP statement documenting all the purchases made during the year and how many shares you were able to acquire.

Be sure these statements are in a safe place. You'll need them for tax purposes when you sell some or all of your shares in the future.

The quarterly form shown on the next page is typical of those you'll receive. The back side describes all the pertinent details on the front side, making this statement particularly easy to read. Some statements don't have such a description, but they all look pretty much the same.

Each quarterly DRP statement will have a blank for you to fill in indicating how much money you'd like to invest, if any, that period. In most cases the minimum amount is $25 to $50 (although it can be as low as $10) with a typical maximum of $3000 to $5000 and more per quarter. In our example that option is at the bottom of the statement (lower right corner) with a range of $25 to $1000 per investment. Believe it or not, there are companies that have no maximums. You could almost drive a Brinks truck up to the front door, unload a million dollars or more, and say, "Here's my money. Buy me more shares."

These quarterly statements are your personal calls to action to send in more money (unless you sign up for bank drafts) to buy more shares, thus increasing your ownership in every company you own, which is the whole purpose of investing wisely.

Let's say you've made your one-share purchases of five companies and are saving $50 a month. After three months you'll have saved $150. Mail that to company 1, using its DRP statement. After three more months you'll have saved another $150. Mail that amount to company 2. The next $150 saved goes to company 3, then to 4, and finally to 5. By this time, 15 months have elapsed and you've acquired an additional $750 of stock in five companies on top of your initial investment. Now it's time to mail your next quarterly savings to company #1 and start the process all over again. We hope you'll be bumping up the amount to $60 a month, then to $70, and so forth, as your income rises. This will enable you to become a multimillionaire even faster.

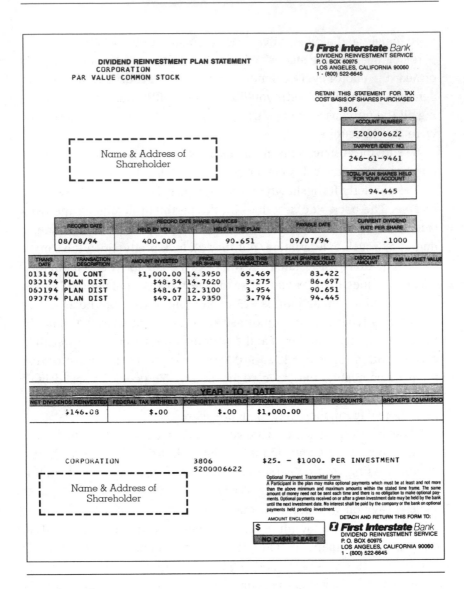

If you change addresses, be sure to notify all your companies. There's a place on the quarterly DRP statement to do that.

In the case of Tate and Whitney, we bought one share each of five companies for them through our broker. Once the shares were received and the children were signed up for the DRPs, we mailed roughly $500 apiece to all the companies to buy additional shares through their no-cost optional-cash-payment plans. The commissions saved by bypassing the broker and dealing directly with the companies immediately went to work for our children.

Naturally, some stocks perform better than others in any given year. To keep the portfolio in balance (20 percent of your money in each company if there are five companies, 16.7 percent if there are six, 14.3 percent with seven, 12.5 percent with eight) it will be necessary to invest more in the laggards and less in the leaders, but that's simple enough to do. If one stock is worth $2000 and the other is worth $2500, you'll need to invest an extra $500 in the former to make it equal to the latter. Don't make the mistake of sending more money only to your top stocks. Portfolio balance helps shield you from fluctuations in the stock market.

Step 5: Sell Only When You Need the Money or When a Company Is Dropped from *America's Finest Companies*®

The majority of investment books proffer one exotic technique or another for selling a stock and switching to another. We don't advocate selling unless it's necessary because you'll have to pay federal and probably state taxes on the gain unless your stocks are in a retirement plan.

Assume you have a $1000 profit on a $1000 initial investment, for $2000 in total market value. If you're in the 35 percent combined-tax bracket, Uncle Sam and the state where you live will take $350, leaving you with $1650. (Children's tax rates are much lower.) The $1650 will have to increase by 21 percent just for you to get back to the $2000 you had ($2000 divided by $1650) before you took a profit. That's about two good years of normal stock-market gains, longer than that if stock prices are sluggish.

The best reason for selling is that you need the money. The next best reason for selling is because one of your companies is no longer in our *America's Finest Companies*® directory, which comes out every June. (We drop a stock if it doesn't have higher dividends compared to the year before.)

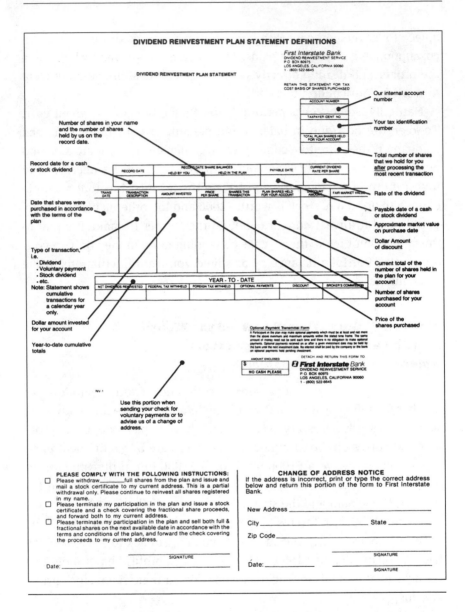

When you sell because you need or want money, sell the stock or stocks with the least profits to reduce the bite from the capital-gain tax.

If you own between five and eight companies, our guess is you'll have at most only one deleted from our list every five years or so because a company fails to increase its dividend.

How do you sell? The original shares you bought from your broker have to be sold through a broker. The company won't sell them for you. For selling all your other shares, use the quarterly DRP statement. Just follow the instructions on the statement, as shown on the next page.

You will be instructed to indicate on the statement how many shares you'd like to sell and mail it back to the company. The company will combine your sell order with all sell orders from other DRP participants and mail you your portion of the net proceeds. Since companies buy and sell in bulk, they're able to pass these transaction savings on to you. Once you submit your sell order, you can expect a check within about two weeks.

In a few cases the company won't sell your DRP shares for you. (That information will be disclosed in the dividend reinvestment packet you received.) Instead, it will mail you a stock certificate for all the whole shares in the plan and a check for the value of the fractional share. If this happens, mail your broker the stock certificate and let him or her sell the shares for you.

To review, the eight principles below are your and your family's worry-free personal map to your financial gold mine:

1. Create your own personal portfolio of at least five to eight of *America's Finest Companies®*.
2. Make sure each company is in a different industry.
3. Invest the same dollar amount in each company to achieve diversity.
4. Buy more of what you already own at least once each year as long as it's still in *America's Finest Companies®*. When a company is deleted, sell and replace it with another company in *America's Finest Companies®*.
5. Stay fully invested.
6. Reinvest all dividends.
7. Sell only when you need the money or when the company is delisted.
8. Be patient. The longer you invest, the more successful you'll be.

Get Ready.
Get Set. Go!

In creating at least a small portfolio of *America's Finest Companies®* for you and each family member, you are doing far more than buying pieces of paper that change in price many times each day. You are actually buying pieces (shares) of U.S. enterprises, some of America's finest, and becoming a part owner. As they grow and thrive in the future, so will you by virtue of your ownership.

Does it really matter if the value of your shares goes down today and then bobs up tomorrow? Of course not. Value can take years to build. Daily fluctuations in stock prices don't mean a thing except that if the stocks go down, you can buy more shares on the cheap. Ignore the media reports you hear. They do not affect the long-term value of the finest American companies. Millionaires don't become millionaires overnight unless they inherit the money or marry into it. What are your chances of doing either of those things?

What does affect the value is growth in the revenue, earnings, dividends, and asset values of the companies you own. If you add to your portfolio of first-rate companies continually, you can rest assured that over the years the value will increase faster than that of all other investments—and keep you well ahead of inflation and the tax man too.

The next step is up to you. You now have the knowledge to convert $50 a month into a million dollars and more. Epicurus warned, "Life is wasted in procrastination." Don't procrastinate. Start your personal road to wealth today!

Happy worry-free investing!

It's easy to make numbers look good on paper, but we came up with a table that shows a fairly typical household income and various saving percentages earning the historical rate of 13 percent a year in stocks, the rate since World War II. Again, we believe that investing exclusively in *America's Finest Companies*® will produce superior returns regardless of what the stock market does. (For this table we assume that household income rises 4 percent each year.)

As an example, a 35-year-old who saves 5 percent of his or her income each year through age 65, with the money returning 13 percent annually and growing tax-free in a retirement plan, would end up with $897,078.

If the amount of household income saved each year rose to 7 percent of income, the end amount would be $1,255,909. At 10 percent a year saved (believe it or not, there are a lot of Americans who save that much and more), the end amount swells to $1,794,156. And if savings rises to 15 percent each year, the end number is $2,691,235.

Please look at the table below. We are assuming starting household income of $35,000 at age 35, which grows 4 percent annually, finally making it to $113,519 by age 65. The total pretax earnings over that period would be $2,076,492. By saving 5 percent of that amount every year, a person would earn an additional 43.2 percent of his or her income. If that person saved 7 percent, it would climb to 60.5 percent of "lifetime" earnings. At a 10 percent savings rate, 86.4 percent; and at 15 percent, 129.6 percent.

Age	Income Grows 4%	Invest 5%/Year	Earn 13% Pretax	Invest 7%/Year	Earn 13% Pretax	Invest 12%/Year	Earn 13% Pretax	Invest 15%/Year	Earn 13% Pretax
35	35000	1750	1978	2450	2769	4200	4746	5250	5933
36	36400	1820	4291	2548	6008	4368	10299	5460	12874
37	37856	1893	6988	2650	9783	4543	16771	5678	20964
38	39370	1969	10121	2756	14169	4724	24290	5906	30362
39	40945	2047	13750	2866	19250	4913	33000	6142	41249
40	42583	2129	17943	2981	25121	5110	43064	6387	53830
41	44286	2214	22778	3100	31889	5314	54667	6643	68334
42	46058	2303	28341	3224	39678	5527	68019	6909	85024
43	47900	2395	34732	3353	48625	5748	83357	7185	104196
44	49816	2491	42062	3487	58887	5978	100949	7472	126186
45	51809	2590	50457	3627	70640	6217	121097	7771	151372

Age	Income Grows 4%	Invest 5%/Year	Earn 13% Pretax	Invest 7%/Year	Earn 13% Pretax	Invest 12%/Year	Earn 13% Pretax	Invest 15%/Year	Earn 13% Pretax
46	53881	2694	60061	3772	84085	6466	144146	8082	180183
47	56036	2802	71035	3923	99449	6724	170484	8405	213104
48	58278	2914	83562	4079	116987	6993	200549	8742	250686
49	60609	3030	97849	4243	136989	7273	234839	9091	293548
50	63033	3152	114131	4412	159784	7564	273915	9455	342394
51	65554	3278	132672	4589	185741	7867	318413	9833	398017
52	68177	3409	153772	4772	215280	8181	369052	10226	461315
53	70904	3545	177768	4963	248875	8508	426643	10636	533304
54	73740	3687	205044	5162	287062	8849	492106	11061	615132
55	76689	3834	236033	5368	330446	9203	566478	11503	708098
56	79757	3988	271223	5583	379712	9571	650936	11964	813670
57	82947	4147	311169	5806	435636	9954	746805	12442	933506
58	86265	4313	356495	6039	499092	10352	855587	12940	1069484
59	89716	4486	407908	6280	571071	10766	978979	13457	1223724
60	93304	4665	466208	6531	652691	11197	1118898	13996	1398623
61	97036	4852	532297	6793	745216	11644	1277513	14555	1596891
62	100918	5046	607198	7064	850077	12110	1457274	15138	1821593
63	104955	5248	692063	7347	968888	12595	1660952	15743	2076190
64	109153	5458	788199	7641	1103478	13098	1891677	16373	2364596
65	113519	5676	897078	7946	1255909	13622	2152988	17028	2691235
Totals	2076492	103825	897078	145354	1255909	249179	2152988	311474	2691235

6

It's Just Too Risky

Some people argue that investing in general, and buying individual stocks in particular, are just too risky, so let's take a close look at risk. In our 2129-page Webster's unabridged dictionary the word *risk* means "the chance of injury, damage, or loss; a dangerous chance; a hazard." To run a risk is "to expose oneself to the chance of injury or loss; to endanger oneself; to take a chance." Let's talk first about risk in the "big picture" of life and then narrow it down to investment risk.

Almost to a man or woman, your favorite politician (assuming you have one) is saying we should "Get tough on crime" because criminals are running rampant in the streets. Illegal drug use among teenagers is growing at an alarming rate after having declined for a number of years. One out of five males (20 percent) is going to get prostate cancer. One in eight women will have breast cancer. That's what we heard on a medical show recently. Some scientists opine that Tylenol and alcohol together are a lethal combination. Johnson & Johnson, which produces Tylenol, disagrees.

Our children are being exposed to one "danger" after another and supposedly are being taught how to avoid those dangers. Schools are teaching drug prevention, rape prevention, sexual harassment prevention, crime victimization prevention, and racial disharmony prevention in addition to all the basic subjects young people need to know. Parents and children alike sometimes are searched randomly when they go into a school and when they attend sports events, not to mention airports. There are regular searches for drugs and weapons. The list expands every year.

What ever happened to the innocence of childhood? The wonders of being young? They're being destroyed faster than the Amazon rain forests. Not only are our children suffering from a megadose of fear, adults, both as citizens and as investors, are suffering as well. And much of it is for naught.

Now back to the "alarming" dangers of prostate and breast cancer and other ailments. Sixty million Americans have high blood pressure, while 2 million are manic-depressive. Another 2 million are schizophrenic. Twelve million have asthma, and 4 million have developed Alzheimer's disease. One in three of us is obese. Is anyone out there healthy and happy? Would both of you please raise a hand?

The numbers above are not facts. They are extrapolations (some of them terribly done), but the media make it sound like they've been handed down from on high. Most things people see doctors for are not recorded on systematic, let alone national, basis. So how does anyone really know about all these sick people who appear to be everywhere?

Okay, if the truth isn't available, a ballpark guess will be good enough to make the headlines. The more extreme the guess, the better the headline. You get the picture. Anybody arguing for anything will try to make his or her side look as statistically compelling as possible. If you want to get funds for prostate research, cite the one-in-five figure. That certainly gets Bill's attention.

But that's not reality. Here's what is. According to the *Wall Street Journal*, the "accumulated risk [of prostate cancer occurs] over some 80 years of life. Put in a kinder, gentler way, if you are 40 years old, your chance of simply getting (not dying of) prostate cancer in the next 10 years is one in 1000. Over the next 20 years, it is one in 100—less than your chance of getting lung cancer. Even by the time you are 70, your chance of getting any kind of cancer, including prostate, is only 1 in 20."

These statistics look a lot different from the story about prostate cancer that recently graced the pages of *Time*, in which the odds of the cancer were vastly overblown. We have to watch out for the words "may be linked," not only in health but in other areas too, because everything might at some level be linked to everything else.

There seems to be more interest today in risks of all types, including investment risks, than at any other time. Lightning-fast computers and bloated databases of all kinds beckon oddsmakers to spew out the probability of something bad happening. It's ironic, we think, that few people see the odds on anything good such as the fact that cars are safer now than ever or that the holes in the ozone layer over both poles are closing or that your chances as an individual investor are actually better than they are when you turn your money over to most professionals (including mutual funds), particularly when you invest for 10 years or longer.

The point we are making is that risks in investing, as in so many areas, are perceived to be much greater than they are. For example, tragic events such as a plane crashing and killing 350 people stand out in people's minds. That number of people die every three days in auto accidents, yet nobody makes much of a stir about it. Likewise, the stock market's great crash of 1987 was a spectacular, once-in-a lifetime sell-off, but millions of investors sold their stocks, remained on the sidelines, and missed one of the greatest stock-market rises in history.

In World War II President Franklin Roosevelt observed that the only thing we have to fear is fear itself. When it comes to managing your money, it is certainly wise to be prudent but to be unnecessarily fearful is counterproductive.

THE PSYCHOLOGY OF INVESTING

Most people have never heard of the Princeton psychologist Daniel Kahneman or his now deceased research partner Amos Tversky, yet the two (especially Kahneman) have done more to explain why people behave the ways we do in various facets of life and in particular in investing than anyone else. They've researched areas ranging from what drives entrepreneurs, to what affects automobile drivers, to what motivates basketball players on a hot shooting night.

In terms of every action a person takes, that person is always making a choice. Should I do it or should I not do it? Each one of us makes this decision hundreds of times every day and seldom realizes he or she is doing it, and in virtually all instances we are subject to thinking we know more than we do. We often act out of overconfidence, but emotion, fear, greed, hindsight, and clouded foresight also come into play. Our decisions frequently are based on what we believe and want rather than on what we know and need, especially in the area of money and finances. Our psychology determines our decision making and personal and business performance. We wrote this book to help you improve your decisions about family finances.

In the realm of personal finances and investing Kahneman and Tversky in 1979 developed a concept called prospect theory, which they later renamed loss aversion. In a nutshell, their research proves that the pain of a financial loss is several times greater than the satisfaction of a financial gain. Therefore, nonprofessionals and professionals alike generally will go to greater lengths to avoid realizing a monetary loss than they will to lock in a monetary gain. That avoidance sometimes involves even greater risk.

> *It ain't so much the things we know that hurts us.*
> *It's the things we know that ain't so.*
> —Artemus Gordon, *Wild Wild West*

A simple example is the 1990s mania involving hundreds of dot-com stocks, most of which ultimately turned into dot-bombs. Companies with clever names, no solid business plan, no earnings, and paltry revenue would offer their shares to a greedy public (the pros were sucked in as well) that saw the stocks keep going up in price. Value didn't seem to matter.

All was well for a few years, until March 2000, when the bubble burst and those stocks began to slide in price. The further they declined, the more people didn't want to sell their shares and "realize" a loss even though they already had a loss.

Let's say Dot.Bomb reached $100 a share in March 2000, the month the NASDAQ index closed above 5000 for the first time. By May 2000 Dot.Bomb could easily have dropped to $70 because when those stocks went over the peak, it was like an avalanche on the downside. If the investor kept the share, he or she had a $30 "unrealized" loss because the stock had gone down that much in value. If the share had been sold, there still would have been a $30 loss, but it would have been captured for tax purposes (a deduction). There also would have been the opportunity to shift into a high-quality company to start to recoup that loss.

The "paper" or "unrealized" loss doesn't seem real to the majority of investors, whereas selling the shares, which is the same "real" dollar loss, is painful. What's the difference? A $30 realized loss is the same as a $30 unrealized loss. It's just that somehow selling the losing share feels a lot worse than holding it and hoping for a recovery. In the case of the dot-bombs, people held on far too long and lost the bulk of their money or all of it as dozens and dozens of those companies went bankrupt.

The Kahneman and Tversky duo showed us that if we recall something easily, we think it happened more often than it did, particularly if it's bad, such as a plane crash or a severe stock-market decline. They also demonstrated that the most recent short-term information is typically the source of long-term money and investment decisions.

Other conclusions we can form from their work include the following:

1. Watching the stock market and the stocks in your portfolio all the time and noticing every blip in the economy is a bad idea.

2. Trying to time moves into and out of stocks (trading) produces mediocre results at best.

3. The long-term future of stocks and stock returns is a lot more certain the further out your time horizon is.

4. Chasing huge returns, such as buying last year's hottest stock or mutual fund, typically results in huge losses.

5. A corollary is that recent returns and performance say nothing about future returns and performance. Kahneman explained that if eight people each have a coin-flip chance to beat the market each year, after three years there ought to be at least one who beat the market all three times solely on the basis of the law of probabilities. That person would look supersmart, wouldn't she? But her superior performance would just be the result of statistics.

6. Nobody can forecast the economy or the stock market accurately because there is no "foreseeable" future.

7. Investors are disposed to hanging on to losing stocks and selling their winners early; study after study proves that.

8. It doesn't matter that one of your friends may be making more money with his investments than you and your family are; what counts is what you and your family do that's in line with your needs, wants, knowledge, and abilities.

When you look at the typical "financial pyramid" that shows up in so many financial-planning books, stocks are up near the top in risk whereas government bonds and banking accounts reside at the bottom. We don't know who drew this pyramid, but it isn't exactly correct when you take into account the full definition of risk.

If you invest in U.S. government bonds, which are widely known as the world's safest and most liquid security, you're assured by Uncle Sam of getting 100 percent of your principal and interest. We think that all but the most rabid doom-and-gloomers would agree with that statement. In contrast, when you buy shares of companies, regardless of their quality, there's always a chance that one or more will go under. (If you have a diversified portfolio of *America's Finest Companies*®, the cream of American industry, the odds of the whole thing going bust are virtually zero. Many of these companies easily survived the Great Depression.)

Putting your money into a bank account is also considered to be 100 percent safe because the banking system is backed up by the Federal Deposit Insurance Corporation (FDIC). Buying the bonds of highest-quality companies such as Exxon Mobil and General Electric is thought to be almost 100 percent safe since the financial strength of those companies and many more like them is impeccable. But after taxes and inflation you'll be behind the eight ball.

> *I'm not so much concerned with a return on my*
> *investment as I am with the return of my investment.*
> —Will Rogers

That brilliant investor Will Rogers opined that he didn't want to lose any of his original principal. Neither does anyone else we've ever met, yet that's exactly what millions of people do when they plop their hard-earned dollars into a bank, buy corporate or government bonds, or buy investment products from an insurance company. In all these cases they are lending their money to the bank, the corporation, the government, or the insurance company. Those entities take the lenders' (aka investors') money, use it for their own purposes, and pay a fixed rate of return. (Some insurance products pay a variable return.)

If you have money in a bank account earning 3 percent interest each year, the bank assumes (and it's almost always right) it can earn more than what it's paying you on your money. Ditto for corporations that issue bonds and insurance companies too. They keep the "spread" between what they can earn and what they have to pay you. Their goal is to pay you the least you'll take and earn as much as they can with your money. The more they're able to do this, the wider their spread and thus the more profits they make.

There is nothing wrong with this. You make money, and they make money too. The problem is that you're a lender, and lenders don't make nearly as much as owners. Lenders have far more difficulty keeping ahead of inflation and taxes than owners do. History proves it.

Let's say you earn 5 percent (this is somewhat above the historical norm) annually in your bank account for each of the next 20 years. Let's also assume that inflation is 4.4 percent a year, the same as it's been since 1945, and that you're in the 25 percent combined tax bracket, which may be low. This is what your earnings will look like from your bank investment:

Interest	5.00%
Less: taxes	1.25% (25% x 5%)
Less: inflation	4.40%
Net return	−0.65%

After taxes and inflation take their bites, you'll actually lose ground to the tune of −0.65 percent a year.

Now look at the same example using *America's Finest Companies'* 13 to 15 percent annual return. Your net return would be 7.35 percent to 9.35 percent. That's quite a difference compared with −0.65 percent, a

Reflections on Risk

To laugh is to risk appearing the fool.

To weep is to risk appearing sentimental.

To reach out for another is to risk involvement.

To expose feelings is to risk exposing your true self.

To place your ideas, your dreams, before the crowd is to risk their loss.

To love is to risk not being loved in return.

To live is to risk dying.

To hope is to risk despair.

To try is to risk failure.

But risks must be taken, because the greatest hazard in life is to risk nothing.

The person who risks nothing does nothing, has nothing, and is nothing.

He may avoid suffering and sorrow, but he simply cannot learn, feel, change, grow, love, live.

Chained by his certitude, he is a slave; he has forfeited freedom.

Only a person who risks is free.

positive difference you can bank on for your secure financial future. Fortunately, that's what *Worry-Free Family Finances* is all about: helping you and everyone in your family be wise with money.

STOCKS ARE THE FINEST INVESTMENT

Perhaps no one has done a finer job documenting the long-term benefits of owning shares of companies than Dr. Jeremy Siegel at the Wharton School. His third edition of *Stocks for the Long Run* (from our publisher, McGraw-Hill) has been updated to show 200 years of financial-market returns. Siegel says, "The stock market is the driving force behind the allocation of the world's capital. Stocks hold the key to enriching the lives of all peoples everywhere." The last dozen words are paramount to our case for owning shares of high-quality companies, in particular our *America's Finest Companies®*.

Stocks historically have made more money than any other investment, including real estate. Siegel says stocks are the number one
investment choice and, surprisingly to many people, are not nearly as
risky as bonds and cash: "Over the long run, the returns on stocks are so
stable that stocks are actually safer than either government bonds or
Treasury bills [cash]."

Stocks are the greatest protection against rising prices. They've grown
three times faster than the rate of inflation since World War II. By putting your money into shares of *America's Finest Companies*®, you will
stay safely ahead of inflation.

One nice thing about Siegel's book is that there are a number of
easy-to-read tables and charts that make the way stocks build substantial personal wealth come to life, several of which are reproduced here.
The chart shown below demonstrates the 200-year returns from
investable assets—stocks, bonds, Treasury bills, and gold—compared to
the annual rate of inflation.

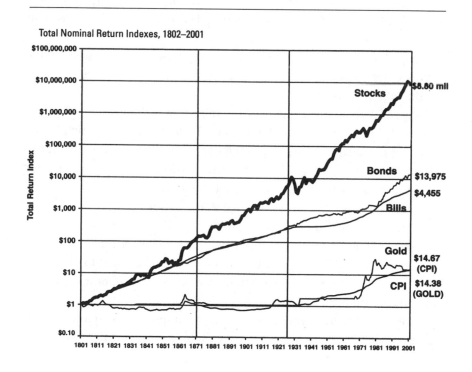

Total Nominal Return Indexes, 1802–2001

Because of an uncertain domestic and worldwide economy at the moment, many investors are turning to gold, which supposedly is a "safe haven" in times of turmoil. The long-term record shows this is not the case. One dollar invested in gold in 1801, when Thomas Jefferson was in the White House, grew to only $14.38 at the end of 2001, two centuries later. Meanwhile, the consumer price index (CPI) climbed to the equivalent of $14.67. Thus, for 20 decades gold failed to keep up with the cost of living.

One dollar invested in so-called safe investments—government-issued Treasury bills and bonds—grew to $4455 and $13,975, respectively. These are compound annual rates of return of 4.29 percent and 4.89 percent. Stocks, in contrast, rose in value to $8,800,000, a compound annual return of 8.23 percent per year.

Siegel notes that after inflation is taken out, stocks (this is all stocks in general, not the "select" list we work from) still returned an annual gain of nearly 7 percent per year for 200 years. On average, this is the equivalent of an investor's purchasing power doubling in value roughly every 10 years. If you break it down further, the after-tax (real) return on stocks was 7.0 percent annually from 1802 through 1870, 6.6 percent from 1871 through 1925, and 6.9 percent ever since. These are incredibly consistent returns any way you look at them.

Siegel has documented that over varying periods of time stocks have consistently outperformed both bonds and Treasury bills (see the table on the opposite page).

Since you and your family ought to invest for as long a period as possible, it is important to note that the last 30-year period in which bonds beat stocks ended in 1861, just as the Civil War began. More important, Siegel's research (along with our own) confirms that the longer your investment horizon is, the more certain your returns are. An analogy is that your local weather forecaster will have better odds predicting how many days it will rain over the next five years than on how many it will rain over the next two weeks. Why? Because the longer the horizon, the greater the probability that the law of averages will come into play. And the law of averages says very clearly, "Stocks beat all other investments over longer periods of time."

Sure, you may be a whiz at investing in antiques, real estate, art, rare coins, ostrich farms, or whatever. But there is no investment we know

Holding Period	Time Period	Stocks Outperform Bonds	Stocks Outperform T-Bills
1 Year	1802-2001	61.0	61.5
	1871-2001	60.3	64.1
2 Year	1802-2001	65.3	65.3
	1871-2001	65.6	69.5
5 Year	1802-2001	70.9	74.0
	1871-2001	74.0	77.1
10 Year	1802-2001	80.1	80.1
	1871-2001	82.4	84.7
20 Year	1802-2001	91.7	94.5
	1871-2001	95.4	99.2
30 Year	1802-2001	99.4	97.1
	1871-2001	100.0	100.0

in which you and anyone in your family can become part owner of some of the finest companies on the planet with as little as $50 to begin and as little risk as these thoroughbreds of America industry offer. Nowhere!

LESSONS FROM AMERICA'S WEALTHIEST INVESTOR

Much investment wisdom distilled through the ages is now available to all of us who want to be better stewards of our money by investing wisely. Warren Buffett has said that he learned a lot from reading Benjamin Graham's *Intelligent Investor* when he was only 19, a useful book that's still in libraries and bookstores everywhere. Buffett acknowledges that there were three key lessons he distilled from Graham, who was one of his professors at Columbia University.

Lesson 1: When you and your family invest in stocks, look at it as if you would want to own an entire business at its current price but can purchase only a portion of it: 1 share, 10 shares, 100 shares, whatever. Investing in solid companies, especially those which hike their cash dividends each year, is much more substantial than worrying about

From the noted British economist and historian John Maynard Keynes:

Lord Keynes gave exemplary reasons for the causes of the Great Depression and how it could have been prevented. Before his death he said, "Investors may be quite willing to take the risk of being wrong [i.e., speculating] in the company of others, while being much more reluctant to take the risk of being right alone." Keynes noted to a friend who thought he'd spotted a market bottom, "Markets can remain irrational longer than you can remain solvent." Words of wisdom from a true expert.

day-to-day fluctuations in stock prices, which you can't do anything about even if you wanted to.

Lesson 2: Mr. Market, that is, the overall stock market, is going to do what it wants to do in the short term regardless of what you do. Think about it this way. Have you ever been stuck in traffic and gotten really tense because of it? Well, the traffic doesn't care how you feel. It is going to do what it has to do regardless of your feelings or opinions. The same is true of investing wisely. Set a steady course and ignore the day-to-day or sometimes even year-to-year fluctuations. Chart you and your family's course and stick to it!

Lesson 3: Margin of safety. Years ago Buffett interpreted this precaution as meaning that when you build a bridge that will hold 40,000 tons, never march more than 10,000 tons across it. In other words, invest with the thought of first not losing money. If you don't lose money, you're sure to make it, and that's the strength of *America's Finest Companies*®, some of which Buffett owns all of or at least part of. In fact, most of the income his company, Berkshire-Hathaway, derives comes from companies that are still in our universe, such as Coca-Cola, or that he has acquired 100 percent of, including Geico Insurance and General Re.

Buffett has said that individuals who believe in the future of American business and are willing to extend a little bit of effort on their own will exceed the results of many investment professionals. He notes, "It's [investment] the only industry I can think of where the professional's efforts subtract value from what the layman can do himself [and of course herself]."

DON'T BUY STOCKS. BUY BUSINESSES.

Here's another perspective on our wealth-building techniques by the financial writer James Glassman. This piece is excerpted from The *Washington Post* (March 17, 2002).

"When people ask me what stocks to buy, my answer sounds flippant, but I'm dead serious: Buy the stocks of the best companies. Or, to put it simply, buy the best businesses.

"As simple as that exhortation sounds, many investors ignore it. They buy stocks they consider cheap or shares that are shooting up in value. I am tempted to ban the word 'stock' from investing vocabularies. Instead, think of yourself as becoming a partner in a great business.

"How do you find such a business? Work backward. Almost always, a great business will have a long-term track record of rising earnings and (if it pays them) rising dividends. A business that can increase its profits consistently is a business that must have a powerful advantage over its competitors—a protective moat that keeps the enemy at bay. A moat can be a great brand name or reputation, or a special way of doing business, or a series of patents. If you can't find the moat, don't worry. Rising long-term profits are a clear signal that the moat exists.

"Luckily, there's another way. Since 1991, Bill Staton, a financial adviser and analyst in Charlotte, has been publishing an annual compendium of what he calls *America's Finest Companies*® (www.billstaton.com, 704-365-2122). To deserve a spot on the list, a company has to have increased its earnings or its dividends for the past 10 years in a row.

"What distinguishes Staton's list is moderation. With few exceptions, the businesses just keep growing, slowly but surely, year after year.

"For those of us who enjoy buying individual stocks, keeping our eye on the ball means focusing on proven businesses—companies like the ones that Bill Staton has so graciously identified for us."

COMPANIES WITH RISING DIVIDENDS
MAKE THE MOST MONEY

Dividend-paying companies make more money than do those which pay nothing at all. Two professors at Babson College and the University of Georgia found that investors are better off, especially in down (bear) markets, with companies that pay dividends. Their research proved that over the previous three decades the average stock paying a dividend (whether it's being increased, decreased, or stagnant) provided a return double that of the companies that did not pay dividends.

A lot of smart people opine that dividends don't matter: It's growth that counts. Another study, this one from investment firm Legg Mason, makes the case for dividends brilliantly. They studied the S&P 500 all the way back to 1973 and included all stocks added to the index, plus all those evicted. Legg Mason found that during that nearly 30-year period the stocks paying dividends greatly outdistanced those that didn't by about a 2-to-1 margin.

Since the S&P 500 (which represents about 80 percent of the total value of all U.S. stocks) index started at the end of 1925, $100 invested grew to roughly $10,000 from price appreciation alone. But with dividends reinvested, the current amount would be approximately $250,000, 25X more. Said another way, price appreciation accounted for only 4 percent of the gain. The other 96 percent came from dividends.

Look at the table below showing the S&P 500's annual returns. You'll note that during periods ranging from 10 to 50 years, dividends constituted no less than 14 percent to as much as 31 percent of the annual total.

	Appreciation	With Dividends	% Return from Divid
1990–2000	14.9%	17.3%	14
1980–2000	12.0%	15.4%	22
1970–2000	9.3%	13.0%	29
1960–2000	8.1%	11.8%	31
1950–2000	8.7%	12.5%	30

Even if we assume that dividends were taxed at the combined 50 percent rate during any of the five periods above, in a taxable account an investor still would have made more money than he or she would have from price appreciation alone.

Many advisers shun higher-yielding stocks for high-tax-bracket investors because they focus only on how much the government will take of that income. They ignore the historical total-return numbers and the fact that higher-yielding stocks go down less in a bear market. Thus, the overall return of the portfolio—dividends with appreciation—is almost always higher than that from price appreciation alone.

We love this quote from a fund manager: "Dividends add ballast to a portfolio, holding down losses in tough times. Dividends are the only portion of stock return that is always positive. And don't forget that as dividends grow over time so does the annual return on your original investment." This is wisdom particularly worth knowing in these days of accounting scandal after accounting scandal. Companies can always monkey (and always have) with earnings, but either they pay a rising dividend or they don't. Dividends never lie.

Question: Isn't the current investment outlook extremely confusing? I just can't seem to figure out what's going on.

Answer: The short-term outlook (one or two years) is always uncertain. For example, based on the history of the S&P 500 index, any one-year period will be up 67 percent of the time. Translated, this means that over the next five years, three will be up and two will be down. However, we can't be certain which will be which. Over rolling five-year periods, the odds of having a profit at the end of each five-year period rise to about 80 percent.

Since the S&P 500 started as an index at the beginning of 1926, there has never been a losing eight-year period in terms of total return: price appreciation with dividends.

Most important, we can't find any 15-year periods in the twentieth century when (1) stocks didn't provide a positive return while also (2) beating inflation.

You and your family have to be long-term investors (a minimum of five years; 10 to 15 years is even better) and base investment decisions on what you all know, not on what you have to guess about. History is on the side of every investor who's willing to remain patient and stay the course.

America's Finest Companies® (AFC) aren't the finest simply because they have the finest dividend and earnings records. An example: The January 16, 2002, issue of the *Wall Street Journal* cited "the" top-rated companies for social responsibility. Of the top 15, these were the AFC companies along with their rankings: (1) Johnson & Johnson, (2) Coca-Cola, (3) Wal-Mart Stores, (4) Anheuser-Busch, (9) McDonald's, (10) 3M, (13) Target, (14) Home Depot, and (15) General Electric. AFC companies occupy 9 of the first 15 slots.

Here's another example. The December 10, 2001, issue of *Fortune* listed the companies that created the most value for their shareholders. The AFC companies cited in the first 25 were (1) General Electric, (3) Wal-Mart Stores, (5) Pfizer, (6) Citigroup, (7) Johnson & Johnson, (8) Merck, (9) ExxonMobil, (12) American International Group, (13) Coca-Cola, (14) Bristol-Myers Squibb, (16) Philip Morris, (18) Eli Lilly, (19) Procter & Gamble, (20) Home Depot, (21) Abbott Laboratories, and (23) PepsiCo.

The February 24, 2002, edition of the *New York Times* said, "In the 1990's, when stock returns averaged 18.2 percent a year, dividends provided just 2.9 percentage points of that. The remainder came from capital appreciation. Over the long term, though, dividends have provided 4.7 percentage points, or more than 40 percent of the market's average annual return of 11 percent since 1926.

"Consistent dividend payers also have strong long-term records, according to a recent study by Standard & Poor's, analyzing 47 stocks it now recommends that have consistently increased dividends in the last 10 years. It found that they outperformed the S&P 500 from 1991 to 2001, rising fourfold versus threefold for the index."

JUST SAY NO

You might be thinking, But what about stock mutual funds? Annuities? There's a million other investments out there besides individual stocks.

Shouldn't I at least consider those? Here are some convincing reasons why you should just say no. We'll spend the most time arguing against stock mutual funds because they seem like an easy answer to so many people but actually are a great way to lose money.

Just Say No to IPOs

IPOs (initial public offerings) were the subject of a *Wall Street Journal* article a couple of years ago. In sum, during the period from October 1, 1999, through March 31, 2000, the absolute height of Internet mania, Deutsche Banc Alex Brown brought nine issues to market, which on February 28, 2001, were down an average 62.8 percent. J.P. Morgan was next in the slaughter race with an average decline of 58.2 percent, followed by Salomon Smith Barney at 56.6 percent and FleetBoston Financial at 53.1 percent. The list went on to name eight other top firms with losses in the range of 41.4 percent to 6.0 percent. None—let us repeat that, none, not a single one—made money. This proves that getting in on the ground floor results in an early burial, not making lots of money.

Just Say No to Annuities

We know we'll get letters, phone calls, and faxes from investment products salespeople around the country, but nonetheless we have to look at the downside of a red-hot product in today's environment. An annuity is an investment contract, typically with an insurance company or another financial institution, in which the annuitant (investor) receives either a guaranteed fixed rate of return or a variable rate of return that fluctuates with the stock market over a specified period, often life. In return, the annuitant invests a lump sum with the financial institution.

Annuities have been around since at least the days of the Babylonians and originated from the "seven years of feast, seven years of famine" concept. When times were good, farmers stored their grain with "bankers" who supposedly guaranteed them an annual supply of grain when times got bad. Today annuities are peddled everywhere, often to people who see (according to *Worth* magazine) "the power of a tax break" that makes them "behave irrationally."

There are benefits to annuities, including tax-deferred earnings outside a retirement plan, unlimited contributions, special death provisions, and an estate-planning advantage or two. But that's just the good side.

The other side rarely is talked about or, even worse, is ignored. The cons include higher fees than the average mutual fund (they can run one or two percentage points a year higher than the fees for a typical stock fund, which is already close to 1.8 percent and is very high), gains taxed as ordinary income when you make withdrawals, early-surrender charges up to 8 percent of the principal, no "stepped-up cost basis" at the death of the owner as there is for stocks and bonds, and the same 10 percent early-withdrawal penalty found in all retirement plans.

It's difficult for a lot of people to decide between the benefits and the negatives because insurance is generally confusing, and after all, that's what an annuity really is: an investment contract tucked inside an insurance policy. Investors buy the annuity either in a lump sum or in periodic installments.

In variable annuities investors can choose from mutual fund options ranging from conservative to aggressive. The studies we've seen show that the mutual funds in annuities lag their brethren outside annuities. That is not good because in any given year the average stock fund underperforms the market, and so the average stock fund in an annuity underperforms it even more.

If you've already pumped all the money you can into your retirement plan or plans, you don't need to buy an annuity for tax advantages. You could create your own group of low- or no-yielding *America's Finest Companies*® and come out better even on an after-tax basis. Your annual tax burden even in a combined 50 percent tax bracket could be as low as 1 percent a year (annual tax on your dividend income), and so your net return could be between 10 and 12 percent a year, far better than virtually any annuity mutual fund or any other stock fund for that matter. Advantage number one.

You can get the money any time you need it without a penalty, and there's a stepped-up cost basis on your death. Advantages 2 and 3.

You save sales loads, early-withdrawal penalties, and a number of other inflexibilities because there are none. Advantage 4.

Here's what the *Wall Street Journal* had to say on July 2, 2002: "Annuities are actually a lot more complex and have downsides that salesmen may not [make that almost never] mention. The higher fees of most annuities can often cancel out their tax advantages; most annuities lock in investors for years; and annuities saddle heirs with higher taxes, unlike mutual funds or most other investments.

"Because annuity sales are so lucrative, regulators including the National Association of Securities Dealers have expressed concern that many of the sales are transacted merely to generate commissions."

Please take our advice: Just say no to annuities.

Just Say No to Mutual Funds

What should you do with stock mutual funds? You guessed it.

"According to Morningstar [a principal mutual fund tracking service], 96.4% of the professionally managed stock mutual funds were unable to beat the S&P 500 in the past decade ended December 31, 1999."

—Bill Donoghue's *WealthLetter*, September 2000

"For the 10 years through 2000 the average stock fund returned an average 14.67% a year."

—the *Wall Street Journal*, January 8, 2001. Over the same period
the Dow Jones Industrial Average returned 17.80 percent
a year, according to the *Value Line Investment Survey*

"[Stock mutual] funds returned an average 9.9% during the 36 years through year-end 1997. Meanwhile, the Standard & Poor's 500-stock index climbed 11.6% a year, while small-company stocks gained 14.8%, as measured by Chicago's Ibbotson Associates.

—the *Wall Street Journal*, February 27, 2001

"The average investor loses 2 1/2 percentage points of return each year to taxes."

—ad from the Vanguard Group (one of the largest mutual fund
companies) in the *Wall Street Journal*, April 3, 2001

After the smashing success of the Broadway play *Amadeus* in the 1970s, the movie version came out a few years later. The king of Austria frequently would enter a room crammed with his personal advisers and ask a simple question. He would get a variety of answers from all present, shrug his shoulders, and remark, "Well, there it is." Then he'd leave.

In a sense, we feel the same way about stock mutual funds. The evidence speaks loudly for all to hear: "Well, there it is"—poor performance year after year after year after year, made worse by the annual tax bite. Yet millions of Americans continue to pour billions of dollars into stock mutual funds every year as if there were no other way to invest.

Mutual funds have become the most popular way for individuals to invest. There are now in excess of 10,000 different ones, and well over half invest exclusively or almost exclusively in stocks. With so much money on the line and pouring into the equity funds at a record clip, you'd think investors would be more careful about where they put their money. Not so.

They often are lured by the creative advertising of mutual funds that seem to offer so much and in reality frequently produce so little. Thumb through any of dozens of investment publications, including your local newspaper, and you'll see ads for this fund or that. Note how they tout their "outstanding" records.

Warren Buffett and his partner, Charlie Munger, a billionaire in his own right, have long questioned professional money management because you usually end up paying someone fees and expenses (that can eat up as much as 2 to 3 percent of your assets annually, and that's before taxes) to do something you may be able to do as well yourself, if not better.

This is not to say that professional managers aren't trying or that you shouldn't have one. We believe most have a high level of integrity and really try their best, but you want to make certain anyone you hire has your best interests at heart, offers a long track record of success, and is compatible with your money needs.

Pick up any financial magazine or financial newspaper and you'll always see an ad for this or that stock mutual fund touting its supposedly superior returns over certain time periods. But what you see all too often is not what you get.

First, there's the problem of returns versus the stock market indexes, the Dow, and the S&P 500. Research from a number of sources, including *Smart Money* magazine, clearly shows that at least two-thirds of all stock mutual funds fail to equal, much less outdistance, the market. *Smart Money*'s study from fall 2000 covers the previous 35 years, when mutual funds came to the fore as places for people to put money.

Aside from the mediocrity inherent in most stock fund returns as shown by study after study, there's that little burden called taxes. Some wag once said, "Death and taxes are both certain, but death isn't annual." Taxes are, and they can eat a *Jaws*-size hole in your after-tax returns. And that's on top of management fees, trading commissions to buy and sell, and other expenses, all of which come out of your and your family's pockets.

Taxes on mutual funds that invest outside of tax-free (retirement) accounts, and this is where most of the fund money is, take an even bigger toll. *Barron's* says, "The structure of mutual funds makes shareholders liable for taxes on any gains realized by the fund, even if individual shareholders didn't benefit from those profits."

The law says that mutual funds must pay out all gains annually. Many funds distribute them twice a year, and almost all make a distribution late in the year. When a fund sells shares at a profit, you pay the tax if the fund is owned outside a retirement plan. Period.

If you invest in individual stocks, you can sell when you want to. If you own a fund, they sell when they want to. Are taxes a big deal? You bet. In a study of stock funds from 1963 through 1992, the National Bureau of Economic Research found that taxes gobble up 55 percent of a high-bracket investor's return.

The *Journal of Investing* survey for the period 1970–1995 discovered that the typical stock fund gave up 44 percent of its returns to fees and taxes. This means only 56 percent of the annual return, which was generally behind the market in the first place, was passed on to the investors.

The news wasn't good for other taxpayers either. Low-bracket investors surrendered 24.9 percent of their returns, while those in a medium bracket gave away 41.4 percent. These are scary numbers, especially since the funds—even before taxes—underperformed the market.

*Government bureau:
Where the taxpayer's
shirt is kept.*

HERB STEIN

What should you do? In a tax-sheltered retirement plan, taxes aren't a worry. In taxable accounts, if you must own mutual funds, look for those with low turnovers (the funds with more of a buy-and-hold mentality). Average turnover in a typical stock fund is 100 percent of the entire portfolio every year. Avoid funds like that.

Index funds have far less turnover than do most stock mutual funds, and although they never beat the market (because of fees, other expenses, and taxes), they do better than most funds. Whenever you're going to purchase shares of funds, make sure you buy additional shares after they make their annual or semiannual distributions. Check with the funds to find out the distribution dates.

There are still more reasons never to own a stock mutual fund, unless your retirement plan, such as a 401(k) or an equivalent plan, allows you no other investment choices:

1. You don't need to pay a professional to invest for you when you can do it yourself better and cheaper.

2. Mutual fund fees and expenses continue to rise. Multibillionaire John Bogle, founder of the enormous Vanguard family of funds, is on the warpath against rising fund costs. He states, "The fees

keep going up—going up like you're in an elevator." The expense ratio of the average stock fund (money that comes out of the investor's pocket) rose from 1.57 percent at the beginning of 1996 to 1.63 percent six years later. And they appear to be in the same relentless upward trend they've been in for the last two decades.

3. Fund managers generally invest for the short term, whereas all reputable studies prove that long-term investing makes more money.

4. It's difficult to find out what kind of investing philosophy a fund really follows. And if you do manage to find out what that philosophy is, is the fund actually following it? In addition, even if you know who the fund managers are, what can you really uncover about their experience and track records?

5. The number of fund choices of all types is mind-boggling. How can an investor know with assurance which ones are the best when every financial publication ranks them so differently?

6. Most stock-fund managers were high school age or younger during the crash of 1987, the steepest stock-market decline in history. In fact, the experience of the typical manager of a stock mutual fund is around five years.

7. More and more funds are increasing their minimums both to get started and to add to the original investment. It generally takes at least $1000 to begin investing in a stock mutual fund, with minimum increments of $500 or more to add to your holdings. With our methodology, there is no minimum to get started and you can add to your stock portfolio whenever you want to, usually as little as $25 to $50 at a time.

When a stock mutual fund buys and sells constantly, who pays? You, the investor, do. The funds that do the most trading incur the highest costs for investors. The typical fund sells and rebuys about 100 percent of the value of its total assets every year. If a fund has $100 million under management for all of 2003, it will sell and rebuy about 100 percent of that amount, or $100 million.

What does this cost you and other investors in funds? Would you believe 1.7 percent of assets per year? (This figure does not include other fund costs, such as the management fee and sales loads, which are charges to either buy or sell the fund. It also excludes taxes.) That 1.7 percent might not seem like so much in a banner year like most of the 1990s, but what about in a punk year like 1994 or down ones like 2000, 2001, and 2002?

Since the end of World War II, the S&P 500 market index delivered an annual total return of 13 percent (stock price appreciation plus dividends reinvested). With that in mind, let's look at how transactions costs alone (never mind all the other ones or taxes either) have a negative impact on returns.

Let's assume the market returns 13 percent a year through the next 20 years (we never bet against history). A $10,000 investment in the S&P 500 will grow to $115,231. If—and this will be a rare exception—your stock mutual fund happens to equal the market but has average transaction costs of 1.7 percent, your money (again excluding taxes) will grow to $85,094, or $30,137 less. Then throw in all the other expenses, and what do you have? Not much to brag about at home, we're afraid.

Now let's put everything together. Even though some 75 to 85 percent or more of stock mutual funds fail to equal, much less beat, the market, for this example we're assuming that Go-Go Fund matches the market's historical return of 13 percent every year for the next 10 years and that the investment is outside a retirement plan and therefore is taxable.

Go-Go Fund

Pretax annual return	13.0%
Less: management fee	1.0%
Less: marketing expenses	0.5%
Less: commissions, etc.	1.7%
Less: taxes	2.5%
Net return to investor	7.3%

Take this example forward. In the market $10,000 today would be worth $33,946 in 10 years. In Go-Go Fund, after all expenses and taxes are removed, your money would grow to only $20,230, or 40 percent less.

Why invest in a stock mutual fund if you don't have to? We don't know why anyone would.

> *To achieve satisfactory investment results*
> *is easier than most people realize.*
> —Benjamin Graham

Benjamin Graham was introduced reverently as one "who needs no introduction to the readers of this magazine" in the final interview of his life in the October 1976 issue of *Financial Analysts Journal,* from which the following has been excerpted:

What is your view of the financial community as a whole?

"Most of the stockbrokers, financial analysts, investment advisers, etc., are above average in intelligence, business honesty and sincerity. But they . . . tend to take the market and themselves too seriously. They spend a large part of their time trying, valiantly and ineffectively, to do things they can't do well."

What sort of things, for example?

"To forecast short- or long-term changes in the economy, and in the price level of common stocks, to select the most promising industry groups and individual issues—generally for the near-term future."

Can the average manager of institutional [as in mutual] funds obtain better results than the Dow Jones Industrial Average or the Standard & Poor's index over the years?

"No. In effect, that would mean that the stock market experts as a whole could best themselves—a logical contradiction."

Turning now to individual investors, do you think that they are at a disadvantage compared with the institutions because of the latter's huge resources, superior facilities for obtaining information, etc.?

"On the contrary, the typical individual investor has a great advantage over the large institutions" [i.e., stock mutual funds and money managers in general].

In September 1998 *Smart Money* magazine noted that for the previous 35 years just 23 percent of all mutual funds had equaled or exceeded the market. That's as telling a statistic as we know about the poor job most stock mutual funds do for investors.

Stock mutual funds suffered their worst year in three decades in 2001 as more than 8 out of 10 stock funds lost money. It was even worse overseas. The Dow Jones World Stock Index, without the United States, dropped 21.02 percent, its second straight annual decline and the worst single-year performance in the history of the index.

Over both the last 5- and 10-year periods through the end of 2001, U.S. diversified equity funds lagged the S&P 500. For the period 1996–2001, funds generated 8.96 percent a year returns versus 10.70 percent for the market. For 1991–2001, the score was funds 11.34 percent and the market 12.94 percent. Now keep in mind that with the exception of the year 2000, the 1990s was one of the finest decades for stocks in history.

Assuming you owned a "no-load" mutual fund that doesn't charge an "entrance fee" up front, the net return would rise from 6.4 percent to 8 percent. Going one step further and assuming that the mutual fund is in a retirement account (where there are no taxes to pay), the net return would rise to 10 percent, but that still would be a lower return than you'd earn with your own portfolio in a taxable account.

When you manage your own money, you don't pay yourself a management fee, nor do you have to buy and sell a lot, nor do you have any marketing and operating expenses. All the money you don't spend in these areas works for your financial future.

Ditto for taxes. The average stock fund turns over the entire portfolio one or more times each year. This results in an inordinate amount of commissions to the broker and taxes to Uncle Sam and the state where you live.

Using our program, you simply buy five to eight of *America's Finest Companies*® (or as many as you can afford), buy more each year as long as they still qualify to be in our exclusive universe, and sell only when you need the money or when one is deleted. Thus, it's easy for each

The Statons' Top 10 Reasons Never to Own a Stock Mutual Fund

Here are our top 10 (but not only) reasons for never owning a stock mutual fund.

1. In any given year 75 to 85 percent or more fail to equal, much less exceed, the market.
2. Why pay a professional for something you might easily do for yourself better and cheaper?
3. Fees and other expenses are generally outrageous and continue to rise.
4. Taxes eat up a sizable chunk of annual returns, as much as 55 percent for wealthy investors.
5. Fund managers generally invest for the short term, whereas long-term investing makes more money.
6. Studies show that throwing darts to select stocks from the financial pages produces results at least as good as those of the majority of funds, if not better.
7. It's often difficult to find out what kind of investing philosophy a fund really has. And if you do find out, is the fund actually following it? How would you know?
8. There are now more than 5200 stock mutual funds. The choices are overwhelming. How can an investor find out which are the best when every financial publication seems to rank them differently?
9. Most fund managers were in high school during the crash of 1987 and have never experienced a bear market. How will they react in the next one?
10. More and more funds are increasing their minimums both to get started and to add to the original investment.

member of the household to have his or her own personal portfolio and have a hand in picking it, unless of course a child is only a few years old. Certainly when a young person is in the first or second grade, he or she

America's Finest Companies® versus Stock Mutual Funds
Total Annual Stock Return Since World War II in S&P 500 = 13%

	Typical Stock Mutual Fund	Your AFC "Mini"-Fund
Annual return	12.00%	14.00%
Less: sales load	2.00	0.00
Less: management fee	1.00	0.00
Less: other expenses	1.00	0.50
Pretax return	8.00%	13.50%
Less: taxes	(@ 20%) 1.60	(@ 5%) 0.68
Net Return	6.40%	12.82%

is more than capable (with a little help and guidance from the parents) of making intelligent choices.

Our methodology is as close to Warren Buffett's as to anyone else's we know. In our investing program you'll spend about one hour a year; cut loads, commissions, fees, and taxes to virtually zero; have a lot of fun; and double your money every five or six years based on historical returns. What more could any investor want?

With our program you have control and don't have to turn over your hard-earned money to someone else or a group of people you don't even know. Many fund managers tend to speculate, and it's your money they are speculating with, not their own.

SHOULD YOU PAY DOWN YOUR MORTGAGE OR INVEST IN STOCKS?

We're probably asked this question as much as any other not only by newsletter subscribers but also by investors who attend our seminars or read a column we've written.

Our answer is always the same: "Forget paying off the mortgage." Let's say you have a $200,000, 30-year mortgage with a 6.0 percent interest rate and your tax bracket is 30 percent. You have some extra cash and have the option to pay an extra $300 a month as pure principal to help retire the mortgage early. Or you can invest it the way we suggest in these pages.

The after-tax cost of your mortgage is only 4.2 percent (6.0 percent x 70 percent [100 percent less 30 percent tax rate]), and that's fixed for three decades. Thinking about this another way, that's the amount you're "earning" on your incremental $300 a month.

That amount per month invested at 4.2 percent annually over 30 years amounts to $217,560. Now contrast that same money earning 13 percent pretax in a retirement plan such as your 401(k), the historical return from stocks since World War II (we believe *America's Finest Companies*® will do even better given enough time). Since there are no taxes until the money is withdrawn, that $3600 per year will grow to $1,326,194, or $1,108,634 more.

But let's be even more conservative than that. Let's say that $300 a month still earns 13 percent a year in a taxable account but taxes eat up 25 percent of your return. The net return will still be 9.75 percent contrasted with 4.2 percent. Even at that lower rate the $300 a month becomes $648,250.

We have one younger money management client with a $500,000 home with no mortgage attached to it. Suppose he took out a $200,000 mortgage at 6.0 percent. In his tax bracket the after-tax cost of his mortgage would be just 3.6 percent.

If he plunks down the entire $200,000 into a buy-and-hold taxable investment account using our program and yielding 1 percent, his annual tax burden will be 0.45 percent on the dividend income. The net after-tax return will be 12.55 percent. At that rate the $200,000 becomes $6,940,567. Is that a good deal or what?

SOME THOUGHTS ABOUT TAXES

If you've held stocks for more than five years (with gains) in a taxable account and your tax bracket has been 15 percent, the new lower federal

> There is one difference between a tax collector and a taxidermist — the taxidermist leaves the hide.
>
> MORTIMER CAPLAN,
> FORMER IRS DIRECTOR

rate is now just 8 percent. (This change could apply to children's custodial accounts.) Investors in tax brackets 27 percent and higher still pay a 20 percent tax.

Parents and grandparents can give stock held five years and more to children and grandchildren. Then, assuming they are in the 15 percent bracket, the stock can be sold at the kids' tax rate, not that of the adults.

The 2001 Tax Relief Act granted all U.S. taxpayers a larger and growing unified credit to help shelter them against estate and gift taxes. In addition, the top tax rates were reduced. For 2002–2003, the amount excluded from taxes is $1 million; for 2004–2005, $1.5 million; for 2006–2008, $2 million; and for 2009, $3.5 million.

Under current law, anyone dying in 2010 and only in that year will be liable for no federal estate tax regardless of the size of the estate. But the estate tax will be reinstated in 2011 with a unified credit reduction back down to $1 million, unless of course the law is changed again. The unified credit applying to lifetime gifts is still $1 million. Maximum estate-tax rates are falling. In 2003, they are 49 percent; 2004, 48 percent; 2005, 47 percent; 2006, 46 percent. Then they fall to 45 percent for 2007–2009 and will disappear for 2010 and beyond unless the law is changed. If the law is changed, the tax rate will jump up to 55 percent starting in 2011.

13 Simple Things You Can Do to Reduce Taxes

1. Hire the sharpest certified public accountant (CPA) you can find, one who can help you plan to reduce future taxes and also help you eliminate current ones, legally of course.

2. Don't pay taxes twice on reinvested dividends in dividend reinvestment plans.

3. Keep accurate records. Save them in a fireproof, theftproof place.

4. Buy low- or no-dividend growth stocks outside retirement plans.

5. Put all the money you can into retirement accounts for an immediate tax deduction and tax-deferred growth.

6. Form a SEP or Keogh plan for an outside business.

7. Itemize every deduction possible while keeping accurate records.

8. Deduct home energy-conservation costs.

9. Make charitable gifts only of appreciated investments.

10. Form a life insurance trust.

11. Don't take on nondeductible interest expense.

12. Add sales tax to the cost of big-ticket items such as a car.

13. Add improvements to the cost of your home.

DO YOU NEED A MONEY MANAGER?

We've emphasized throughout this book that we believe most people don't need to hire a money manager. We talk to individuals, couples, and corporate executives virtually every day who are considering letting one of our companies, Staton Financial Advisors, LLC, manage their personal and/or corporate money. We'd like to share the pros and cons on whether to use a professional because most individuals and families do not need one.

You can hardly walk across the street anymore without being taxed.

J. PAUL GETTY

The biggest pro is relief from the responsibility of managing your money or your company's money. Few business owners want the fiduciary, much less the potential legal, burden of managing employees' money in a 401(k), profit-sharing, defined-benefit, or other retirement plan. A second pro is that the money can be managed to meet your goals or those of a particular plan. Obviously, a third pro would be equaling or beating relevant benchmarks such as the Dow Jones industrial average and the S&P 500 market index. A fourth pro is not having to spend any of your personal time on investing when there are so many other things you want to do.

The cons are many: (1) managers' inexperience, (2) generally poor track records, (3) unsubstantiated and/or hyped returns, (4) high fees, (5) failing to meet clients' needs, and (6) inaccessibility of the managers.

Having a great relationship is paramount. You have to trust your manager and be very comfortable with how he or she relates to you. Your manager should be accessible to answer all questions and concerns and should contact you regularly to ensure that your financial needs and investment objectives are being met.

How much money do you have to have to hire a money manager? Most have significant minimums ranging from $250,000 to a million dollars and up. Here's a simple quiz that may help you decide.

1. I really enjoy managing my money.
   True
   False

2. I have a good enough investment background to manage my money competently.
   True
   False

3. I don't have fiduciary responsibility for a pension or profit-sharing plan.
   True
   False

4. The time it takes to manage my money is fine with me.
   True
   False

5. I always know what my long-term return has been versus the market.
   True
   False

6. I can accomplish my long-term financial goals without the help of an adviser.
   True
   False

7. I am not overburdened by or overwhelmed with financial information.
   True
   False

8. I always make investment decisions that are based strictly on the facts. No emotions are involved.
   True
   False

9. I am not afraid to sell a losing or low-quality investment.
   True
   False

10. I tend to let my profits build over the long term.
    True
    False

11. There's someone in my family or company to run the portfolios if something happens to me.
    True
    False

12. I pay careful attention to taxes in managing my money.
    True
    False

13. I have not separated or divorced recently.
    True
    False

14. My health is good to excellent.
    True
    False

15. I prefer individual securities to mutual funds.
    True
    False

16. I could financially sustain a substantial drop in my portfolio.
    True
    False

17. I am patient enough to let a time-proven strategy work even though it may be out of favor for several years.
    True
    False

18. I know how to insulate my money from a lengthy bear (down) market.
    True
    False

If you answered true to all 18 questions, you're probably akin to a financial genius and already doing a superb job with your money. If you answered at least 12 of the 18 with a true, you're most likely doing well

I can't be involved in 50 or 75 things. That's a Noah's Ark way of investing - you end up with a zoo that way.

WARREN BUFFETT

with your money, particularly if you answered true to questions 1, 2, 6, 8, 17, and 18. Those questions are critical in our opinion.

The fewer the trues, the higher the probability you may need a personal money manager. If questions 1, 2, 6, 8, 17, and 18 generated falses, you almost certainly need professional help, the monetary kind that is.

THE REAL SECRET TO BECOMING WEALTHY

We'll close with observations from our friend Don Hutson (www.donhutson.com), one of the country's top motivational speakers.

Bill: Don, are you a financial planner, CFP, or ChFP?

Don: No, I'm a student of human motivation and high achievement with a longtime fascination for wealth and individual financial performance.

Mary: You have enjoyed impressive success as a professional speaker and trainer of salespeople and managers. Why such an interest in finance?

Don: I believe measuring financial progress is an excellent way to keep score for a person seeking business success. Additionally, for those with philanthropic goals, the more you acquire, the more you can give away.

Mary: What is the single most important thing you've learned about building wealth?

Don: That increasing net worth is not a function of income. It is a function of strategy and planning. When I started making some money in my twenties, I thought, "This is great—I'll undoubtedly be rich some day." Unfortunately, wealth seldom just shows up on your doorstep. It comes to those who have developed a sound course of action. My plan for wealth building wasn't working very well, primarily because I hadn't plotted a path. When I drew up a disciplined plan, I started making progress.

Mary: What are some other premises you've found to be critical for increasing wealth?

Don: A person must understand his or her lifestyle cost. Most of us have heard for years that the single most expensive thing you'll purchase in your lifetime is a home. I disagree—it's your lifestyle. Compute your total lifetime earnings and from that figure deduct your net worth. The remaining figure is what you've paid, in dollars, for the lifestyle you've experienced. After computing this, most people are astonished. They don't have the lifestyle they think they've bought.

Bill: That's a revealing concept. How should our readers respond?

Don: Make sound single decisions that result in long-term financial gain. Lifestyle may suffer a little at first, but this will give your readers lots of alternatives later.

Mary: What kinds of decisions?

Don: One example is the power of the automatic deduction. Make a decision today, for example, to have $100 a month or more automatically deducted from your savings or checking account and transferred into your stock investment account. When deductions are made without your having to make a decision each month to invest, the work and worry are taken off your back.

Bill: We like simple moneymaking techniques. Why does this one work so well?

Don: Because it is a process that goes on without further involvement from you. It is a terrific example of what you advise your clients to do: take a profitable course of action.

Bill: Are there other ways to capitalize on the "process-in-place" concept?

Don: Sure. You are limited only by your imagination. Last July my wife and I decided to add a new dimension to our investment plan by investing in your *America's Finest Companies*® after subscribing to your advisory. After discussing our choices in depth, we created our process, and it's working great.

Bill: Would you mind sharing the exact investing process you and she decided to use?

Don: Not at all. Twice a month (the first and the fifteenth) we appropriate $800, which we invest religiously in the five stocks we picked from your AFC list (one stock is invested in each time). We never have a discussion like "Are we going to invest the $800?" That decision has already been made. We live with it because (1) it is a comfortable decision and (2) it's the right thing to do. Our investment process is in place and steadily building our wealth.

Mary: Don, before we close, do you have any other pearls of wisdom for our readers?

Don: Yes, one more. The single smartest thing I've done that saved me money and also helped my son was to tell him, at age 15, that I would pay for his college education and give him $5000 cash if he graduated in four years. He did and I paid, and we both won. I knew that only 11 percent of those entering college graduate within four years. The cost of one or two extra years of college would have been far more than the $5000.

THE FINAL WORD

All You Need to Know about Speculation

1. What it is:
   The opposite of investing
   Guessing
   Gambling
   Trying for quick profit.

2. What a famous investor said:
   "There are two times in a man's life when he should not speculate: when he can't afford it and when he can."—Mark Twain

3. What the Statons say:
   "Don't."

BANK ON IT

STEADY PLODDING BRINGS PROSPERITY: HASTY
SPECULATION BRINGS POVERTY.

Proverbs 21:5

7

Preparing for Life after Work

> If I'd known I was going to live this long,
> I'd have taken better care of myself.
> —JAZZ GREAT EUBIE BLAKE ON HIS
> HUNDREDTH BIRTHDAY (HE DIED AT 104)

We'll begin this chapter with an eye-opening chart. If you've ever wondered how little money it takes to become a millionaire, this will show you. Please go through it carefully with your children and/or grandchildren. It's that important!

How Much per Month to Become a Millionaire?
Assumptions:
1. You begin life after work (retire) at age 65.
2. You earn 13 percent annually in your retirement plan (so taxes are not a consideration) based on *America's Finest Companies*®, the program outlined in these pages.
3. You want to end up with $1 million.

Starting Age	Monthly Investment	Annual Investment
16	$19	$228
18	$24	$288
20	$32	$384
25	$61	$732
30	$117	$1,404
35	$226	$2,712

40	$440	$5,280
45	$873	$10,476
50	$1,800	$21,600
55	$4,049	$48,588

Note in the table that it takes only $19 per month (most of us waste much more than that every 30 days) for a child starting at age 16 to end up with a million dollars by age 65 (a total invested of only $11,400 spread out over 50 years). Compare that tiny amount to $440 monthly (23 times more) starting at age 40 and $1800 a month (95 times more) starting at age 50. It is imperative that we all, as parents and grandparents (yes, young as we are, we qualify on both counts), to get our children and grandchildren on a sound investment program as early as possible.

In the case of our grandson, who is less than one year old, we bought stock directly from several different companies listed in this book to get him off on the right foot monetarily. We will continue gifting various amounts of money into his accounts on special occasions such as birthdays and Christmas and encourage his parents to do the same. In addition, we'll do the same thing for him we've done with our four children. Whether we give our grandson money or he earns it, if he uses that money to buy more shares of his companies, we'll match the amount dollar for dollar. Children are very smart. They recognize an easy doubling of their money even before they put it to work.

Inflation is a negative fact of life because the overall prices of goods and services increase over time. For most of history inflation has existed, and we can assume it will be part of our lives in the future. You want to take that into account in planning for retirement (which we prefer to call life after work; otherwise it sounds like you dropped off a cliff and do little, if anything).

We assume that inflation (the cost of living) will increase at 4 percent per year in the future because that's roughly the rate since World War II (the actual rate has been 4.4 percent). At a 4 percent rate the cost of living will double every 18 years, quadruple in 36, and increase 16-fold in 72. Translated, what costs $1000 today will cost $2000 18 years from now, $4000 in 36 years, and $16,000 in 72 years, based on historical inflation numbers for nearly the last 60 years.

How many decades have you got to live? Once you make a stab (guesstimate) at that figure, it's easy to zero in on how much the next 20, 30, 40, 50, 60, or more years will cost using an even 4 percent (to make the calculations simpler) inflation-rate assumption. Of course, that inflation rate could be high, but it also could be low. Our guess is that 4 percent is about on the money for the longer term based on history, and history is the only realistic guide we have.

Life after work might take a lot more money than most people think, especially given that people don't like to reduce their lifestyles and probably will live longer than expected. Wouldn't it be terrible to have plenty of good years left and a zest for life but no money for anything more than the bare necessities?

Having said that, we think the following table will be useful for you and everyone in your family, especially the young people. It shows how long a given amount of money earning a certain rate of return will last. As an example, let's say you have $100,000 earning 10 percent a year and you're going to withdraw $12,000 (12 percent of the beginning principal) each year. Go down the column "Annual Withdrawal Rate" to 12 and then across the "Annual Interest or Growth Rate" row under the number 10. At that intersection is the number 18. That's how many years your money will last.

Annual Withdrawal Rate (%)	Annual Interest or Growth Rate (%)									
	5	6	7	8	9	10	11	12	13	14
6		36								
7		25	33							
8		20	23	30						
9		16	18	22	28					
10	14	15	17	20	26					
11	12	13	14	16	19	25				
12	11	11	12	14	15	18	23			
13	9	10	11	12	13	15	17	21		
14	9	9	10	11	11	13	14	17	21	
15	8	8	9	9	10	11	12	14	16	20

As you near or enter life after work, many financial gurus suggest that you sell a bunch of your stocks and scurry into bonds and cash because that's a "far less risky" money strategy. Although this advice may sound correct, it's often way off the track.

The reason has to do with the term *risk*. The first thing most people associate with risk is buying something that goes down in price. Stocks, for example, are supposed to be much riskier than other assets because they go down in a bear market (bear markets fall; bull markets rise).

But there's another side to risk. For the 50 years through December 31, 2001, the total return from Treasury bills (about what you'd get in a certificate of deposit) was 4.8 percent a year. Inflation was 4.0 percent, and so the net real return (after inflation) was 0.8 percent a year (4.8 percent −4.0 percent = 0.8 percent), not great, but at least it kept ahead of inflation—if taxes are excluded.

With taxes it's a different story. In life after work your tax bracket frequently drops, but when state taxes are taken into account, the combined tax rate can easily be 25 percent or more. How does a 25 percent

Horrible Tax News for Mutual Fund Investors

If you love mutual funds, you'll hate this. According to the Lipper Organization, high-tax-bracket investors in taxable stock mutual funds lost one-third of their gross returns over the last decade to expenses, loads, and federal taxes.

Lipper said that taxable diversified U.S. equity funds returned 12.7 percent a year for the decade through 2001 (less than the Dow and the S&P 500), and expenses and loads further reduced that return to 11.2 percent. Taxes dropped the annual return to just 8.6 percent.

And in the case of load-taxable bond funds, up to 86 percent of returns evaporated—86 percent!

That's horrible any way you slice it!

Source: *Journal of Financial Planning*, November 2002

tax rate hurt? Here's the answer: 4.8 percent return minus 25 percent in taxes = 3.6 percent annual return, minus 4.0 percent inflation = −0.4 percent net annual return. You lose ground to the tune of nearly half a percentage point a year in Treasury bills.

Let's look at this another way. You and your wife are both 70 years old and in good health. Your life expectancy easily could be as much as 15 to 20 more years. Based on the estimated future rate of 4 percent inflation, the cost of living will increase 91 percent to 137 percent during that time.

Inflation is the biggest financial threat to all Americans regardless of age. For a baby born today with a normal life expectancy of 85, the cost of living will rise 28 times before he or she dies, assuming inflation climbs 4 percent annually. If the child lives to 90, inflation will multiply 34 times. What costs $1000 today will cost between $28,000 and $34,000 then.

Retirement plans are a good deal because you get double tax benefits: (1) a reduction of your annual taxable income and (2) tax-deferred growth. Retirement plans such as 401(k)/403(b) plans are even better because the employer generally makes some sort of match, typically 50 to 100 percent on the dollar. For every dollar you put in, your employer typically adds another $0.50 to $1.00. Where else can you make such an outsized return before your invested dollars go to work?

Let's see what a great deal this can be. Suppose in your company's 401(k) the company matches every dollar you contribute up to 5 percent of your income. If that 5 percent is $2000, the company invests $2000 as well—$4000 in total between you and them. Thus, if you got into a really horrible economic and investment environment and your investment fell 50 percent in one year (extremely unlikely), the loss would be the company's contribution of $2000. You still would have your original contribution, and so in actuality you would have lost none of your money.

But suppose the money you contributed earned a very reasonable (we hope conservative) 8 percent a year, which would amount to $160 (8 percent × $2000 = $160) the first year. On top of that, the company's $2000 contribution also earned 8 percent, or $160. Then you would have earned $160 on your money plus $160 on their money for a total first-year return of 16 percent ($320 divided by your $2000). Where else can you get that kind of return with such certainty?

An employer's matching contribution to the typical 401(k) or 403(b), coupled with the tax deferral, almost always makes these plans profitable even in the most severe market declines.

The three worst annual declines in stock-market history were 43.3 percent in 1931, 35 percent in 1937, and 26.5 percent in 1974. Only a handful of other years were worse than 12 percent. The risk of suffering a huge decline in any specific year is extraordinarily small.

Let's go back to December 31, 1930, the eve of the worst annual stock-market smash. There were no 401(k)s then, but let's assume there had been. You face two options: (1) put $1000 of pretax income into stocks through your 401(k) or (2) put $720 after taxes in cash in a vault for ultimate safety.

You choose the pretax investment in your company plan because there's a one-to-one match on your contribution. Thus, $2000 (your $1000 and their $1000) goes into stocks, but only $720 of your money is invested; $280, which normally would go toward your taxes, is tax-deferred and invested for you along with the company's $1000 match. Stocks plunge 43.3 percent, and your $2000 beginning stock portfolio plummets to $1134. At the year's end, although you're severely disappointed, you find that what amounted to a $720 out-of-your-pocket commitment has grown 57.5 percent. That compares with a zero return on your "safe" in-the-vault cash. Even with a 50 percent match from your company, you'd have ended up with $851, $131 more than your "real" contribution.

In any retirement plan, investment choices fall into three broad groups: stocks, bonds, and savings-type accounts. There's no question which of the three a savvy investor should be in.

THINGS YOU NEED TO KNOW ABOUT RETIREMENT PLANS

There are many things about retirement plans most investors don't know. For example, how about an after-tax 401(k)/403(b) contribution once you make the maximum pretax one? Roughly 40 percent of America's largest companies offer this benefit, and the number is growing. The contributions are not tax-deductible, but the money still grows without taxes until it is withdrawn at age 59 $^1/_2$ or beyond. The plan administrator keeps up with all the paperwork. All you have to do is put money in.

If you leave your employer, your after-tax contributions are returned to you tax-free, but they are not eligible for an IRA rollover as are pre-tax contributions.

The standard advice for someone leaving a company or starting his or her own is to take the retirement money and move it into a new plan or roll it over into an IRA. Few people know that they might have another option: leaving their money where it is. A growing number of plans let you leave some of or all of your money with the current employer even after you're no longer there.

Why might you want to do this? First, the returns and investment options in the old plan may be higher than those in the new. Second, you don't have to keep records. Third, company-sponsored programs are virtually judgment- and creditor-proof, and this is very important in case you are sued, the odds of which seem to grow almost every day.

Fourth, if you're working when you turn age 70 $^1/_2$, you don't have to start taking distributions, which is not true if you have one or more IRAs. This alone can be a powerful advantage. Fifth, you usually can borrow money from a company plan, which you cannot do with an IRA.

Now for the downside of these plans. Employers have a lot of lee-way over when they can dispense retirement plan monies. Sometimes it's just a few weeks. Sometimes it can be many months or even years. Also, rules for different age groups may vary. Many employers do a rot-ten job of explaining what those rules are. Our advice: Don't waste another moment. Make sure you know your employer's guidelines as soon as possible. Call and/or visit whomever you need to.

Two additional negatives are excessive fees and lousy returns. *Money* magazine suggests that companies "skim" at least $1.5 billion a year from workers' retirement savings. The magazine goes on to state: "The huge, hidden costs of 401(k)s, which many companies conceal from plan participants even when the fees seriously erode investor returns, amount to America's biggest retirement rip-off."

Up to 2.5 percent of your investment assets may be gobbled up each year by excessive administrative costs and mutual fund management fees, and as *Money* confirmed in a recent survey, you may have to put a full-court press on your employer to find out just how much they are. It's your legal right to know.

Most of these retirement plans still allow you to invest only in mutual funds, which in almost all cases consistently lag the market. But more and more companies are allowing the individual to make his or her own choices of individual stocks, we hope *America's Finest Companies*®. Please find out if you have that choice.

If you can do that, we suggest scrapping your stock mutual funds and redeploying your money into individual stocks from the list we provide on page 122. First, you're almost sure to reap higher returns. Second, you'll save the annual fees that all funds levy.

Please Take More Vacation

Why is it we Americans take less vacation than any other civilized nation? Is it because we really enjoy work so much? We doubt it. President Bush takes working vacations at his 1,600-acre ranch in Crawford, Texas, but he appears to be not working during a good part of that time, which is what vacation is all about.

Study after study shows we all need to give ourselves more time off to prevent heartburn, insomnia, headaches, high-blood pressure, etc. In Europe, four-to-six weeks' vacation a year is practically mandatory, and the workweeks are shorter. Recently a major foreign newspaper said, "The US currently gives workers the stingiest holidays in the industrialized world."

If George W. can take time to relax and enjoy his vacation by cutting trees and reading books, why can't we? Surely our jobs aren't any more stressful than his. Besides, we might actually find we enjoy vacation—and our family life and ability to make money might improve dramatically. Think about it!

One last piece of advice: Check with your tax adviser if you have one. The tax consequences of retirement planning are far more complex than they appear, and the laws are in constant flux, some for the better and some for the worse.

NOW YOU CAN INVEST A LOT MORE FOR YOUR RETIREMENT

Under recent tax-law changes (in which the changes actually helped all Americans), everyone can now set aside more money for life after work through IRA and 401(k) plans.

The annual contribution limit for an IRA is now $3000 versus $2000 in previous years, and in addition there's what's dubbed a "catch-up" amount of an extra $500 for people age 50 or older. Thus, in 2002 the annual maximum contribution limit jumped 50 percent from $2000 to $3000 if you're under 50 and 75 percent to $3500 if you're older than that. And slowly but surely it gets better. Here's a simple table that makes the point.

Year	Limit	Catch-Up	Total
2003	$3000	$500	$3500
2004	$3000	$500	$3500
2005	$4000	$500	$4500
2006	$4000	$1000	$5000
2007	$4000	$1000	$5000
2008	$5000	$1000	$6000

From the table you can see that the maximum allowable IRA annual contribution stays at $3500 for 2003 and the next year. Then it goes up another $1000 in 2005, jumps another $500 for both 2006 and 2007, and moves up again $1000 in 2008 to $6000 per year. The total maximum allowable annual contribution shoots up 71 percent over the next six years.

Now let's take a look at the new legislation for the very popular 401(k)s, which also encompasses 403(b) and 457 retirement plans:

Year	Limit	Catch-Up	Total
2003	$12,000	$2,000	$14,000
2004	$13,000	$3,000	$16,000
2005	$14,000	$4,000	$18,000
2006	$15,000	$5,000	$20,000

Again, we're talking about maximum contributions, but the total possible rises 67 percent between 2003 and the end of 2006. However, there's another plus: Annual increases in maximum contributions are then indexed to changes in the cost of living as measured by the consumer price index.

There are still more bonuses in the new tax law. If you or your spouse owns a business or may be starting one, the 401(k) may actually be attractive for sole proprietors for the first time. In 2002 the most an employer and an employee could save together in a Simplified Employee Pension (SEP) was $30,000 or 15 percent of the first $170,000 of income, whichever was less. There were some technicalities that could have made those amounts even lower.

Now the total maximum SEP contribution is 25 percent of the first $200,000 of income or $40,000, again whichever is less. Since the 25 percent maximum does not include employee contributions, a self-employed person can make the maximum contribution to his or her plan and put another $11,000 ($12,000 if catch-up applies) into a 401(k).

There is just one hitch. The total annual contributions to all plans may not be greater than $40,000, but then, you can't have everything.

A SEP/Keogh Grows Rapidly Even When You Start Late

Age	Annual $ Contribution (Increases 10% Annually and Earns 13% a Year Tax-Free)
50	$10,000
51	$11,000
52	$12,100
53	$13,310
54	$14,641

55		$16,105
56		$17,716
57		$19,487
58		$21,436
59		$23,579
60		$25,937
	Total Contributions	$185,310
	Worth at Age 65:	$1,111,995
	Worth at Age 70:	$2,048,779
	Worth at Age 75:	$3,774,743

PLANNING YOUR ESTATE

The two most desirable estate plans are taking it with you and not going. There are two stages of wealth building: (1) accumulating and (2) disposing. The focus here is on estate taxes and how to get a handle on how much you might owe.

Live Simply with Style is the name of a new website (www.livesimplywithstyle.com) two friends from Tryon, North Carolina, started. They retired when Ford was 43 and Mara was 39. They told us, "We retired without pension plans or a great deal of money. The outcome has been better than anything we could have imagined. The links below might help your thinking. If you want to know more, we've written two books on retirement."

The tips section is especially intriguing with ways to "simplify and gain style, reduce clutter, know when Enough Is Enough, run your own Breakaway experiment, and Time Is All We Have."

We invite you to check it out. There is no obligation on your part. Ford and Mara are two of the nicest people you'll ever meet, genuine in every sense of the word. There's something on their site for just about everyone.

What is your estate? In the simplest terms it's everything you own minus everything you owe. When you deduct the latter from the former, you calculate your net estate, which is where taxes come in. And what is estate planning? It's taking what you have and getting it to the right people while maintaining the standard of living you desire.

Estate taxes are onerous, to say the least. The federal rate starts at 37 percent and quicker than a flash escalates to 55 percent. When you throw in state estate taxes, the highest combined marginal rate can easily exceed 60 percent. You keep 40 percent or somewhat less. The government takes the rest.

Many unwitting millionaires, unaware they have achieved such status,
may not realize it until it's too late to plan properly.
—*Physician's Money Digest*

The only way to reduce federal estate taxes is to reduce the amount of estate subject to tax. To reduce your estate before you die, you can spend it faster than you make it. Or you can transfer some, if not all, through gifts. Estate reduction = tax reduction.

If your net worth is less than $675,000 counting life insurance, you will not pay estate taxes. But what about other costs and time?

If you do nothing, you've already got a will by default: the will of the state where you live. Each state governs asset disposition with its own laws. In general, those laws provide that a person's spouse (or spouse with children) inherits the estate. A single person's siblings and/or parents divide the estate. If there are no heirs, the state gets it all.

One very important reason for a good will and/or trusts is to provide for your children and grandchildren. Keep these documents up-to-date in light of constantly changing financial needs and tax laws.

It's imperative to use an expert in this area, preferably someone who does nothing besides estate planning. A good place to start is your bank's trust department. Ask for the top expert they know and then use him or her. It's worth extra hundreds of dollars up front to save thousands or tens of thousands of dollars later. Estate planning requires solid professional advice. Not just any lawyer will do.

Attorney fees range from a few hundred to several thousand dollars; it depends on the value of your assets and the complexity of the arrangements. Prepaid Legal Plans and similar organizations are popping up across the country to help people cut costs. Fees to manage trusts are generally in the range of 0.75 percent to 1 percent annually. The larger the assets, the lower percentage the fee.

All banks and trust companies provide one excellent advantage: continuity of management. You also must consider their track record of managing others' assets.

There is some good news about estate taxes. Gifts to charity are tax-free no matter how large they are. And one spouse can leave an entire estate, no matter how large, to the other spouse. Estate taxes = zero. But all that does is postpone them.

In addition, every person gets what's called a unified credit, which was worth $650,000 in 1999 and incrementally escalates each year to $1 million in 2006. The credit applies as a reduction to your net taxable estate before taxes kick in.

Remember that your descendants will have to deal with this issue. It's unfortunate, but all the emphasis over the years has been on how to maximize returns on IRAs and other retirement plans with little thought going into the tax consequences once the owner dies.

It is never too early to start planning the disposition of your estate, including your retirement plan or plans. Even though nobody likes to think about dying, getting an immediate handle on your estimated estate-tax burden is worth doing. After all, there's no need to pay Uncle Sam a penny more than you have to.

If you move to another state, have an attorney review your estate plan. And remember that two-thirds of Americans die intestate: with no will. Please don't be among them. Remember, as Woody Allen says, "Your will is your very last chance to have your own way."

INHERITING A RETIREMENT PLAN

If you are going to inherit a retirement plan, you could be stuck with outrageous bills and multiple headaches too.

According to *USA Today*, "During the next two decades, baby boomers will inherit a bewildering array of stocks, bonds, mutual funds, individual retirement accounts, real estate and personal property. Untangling the estates will require an army of financial planners, lawyers, accountants and family therapists."

Roughly $145 billion shifted hands in 2000, nearly double the $84 billion in 1995. Uncle Sam will be there every step of the way, waiting to grab every dollar he can. That can be a major problem if you're not prepared. It might not be a problem at all if you are. The time to get prepared is today.

Let's say you inherit an IRA worth $1 million when your father dies. In the majority of cases the IRA must be distributed to the inheritor within five years of receiving it, at which time it becomes fully taxable at ordinary income-tax rates.

However, if the recipient elects within one year of the owner's death, the distribution can be spread over his or her lifetime. In one example we studied the recipient was age 50 when he received one-third of a million. (One brother and one sister each got the other third.)

Instead of facing more than $120,000 in taxes within five years through forced liquidation of the account, he elected to "annuitize" and take out only the minimum distribution required each year by IRS tables. That was about $6800 the first year. The rest of the money continued to accumulate tax-free.

ESTATE TAXES ARE VOLUNTARY

"Nothing is certain but death and taxes." While that may be true sometimes, this phrase does not apply to estate taxes. With proper planning, they can be voluntary.

In 1976 James Casner, a renowned professor of law at Columbia Law School, stated before a congressional committee, "We haven't got an estate tax. What we have is you pay an estate tax if you want to. If you don't want to, you don't have to." Professor Casner's statement is as true today as it was then. Does it sound too good to be true?

In 1989 *Forbes* was set to list Sam Walton, founder of the Wal-Mart chain, as one of the 400 wealthiest people in America with an estate in excess of $9 billion. But *Forbes* discovered that Walton no longer owned all of Walton Enterprises, the family company controlling all his Wal-Mart stock. In fact, his children each owned 20 percent of the stock (valued at $1.8 billion apiece then), and each was then listed in the top 400. Each member's stock is worth more than $25 billion today.

Forbes was compelled to print a special supplement listing Sam Walton and each of the children. On his death in 1992, stock owned by the children was worth $20 billion. Sam Walton's estate saved a combined total of approximately $11 billion in estate taxes by gifting stock to his children before his death.

How did Sam Walton get to be so smart? He learned from his father-in-law, who'd done the same thing years earlier with a large ranch in Oklahoma, which was passed to Walton's wife and her siblings. Walton decided to do the same thing with his business in 1954, which at the time consisted of only a few variety stores.

Sam Walton believed that he knew the future of retailing and that the stock would appreciate rapidly over the next few years. We bet he was surprised to find that each child's stock (worth about $5000 at the time of the gifts) would appreciate to an estimated value of $5 billion.

Sam Walton is one example of how extraordinarily wealthy people minimize estate taxes or avoid them entirely. Just as we have profited from studying Warren Buffett's powerful investing techniques (and pass them on to you), we can all benefit from studying what the wealthiest people in America do to reduce or escape estate taxes.

Research has uncovered, affirmed, and refined many highly effective estate-planning techniques used by the very wealthy. One is the family limited partnership. Another is the generation-skipping trust, which can avoid estate taxes totally for future generations. These and many other estate-planning techniques are highly effective and sometimes elegantly simple.

By studying and following the lead of the most successful people, you too can minimize or totally avoid estate taxes.

We prepared this section with help from tax attorney and CPA William R. Culp of Culp Elliott & Carpenter, P.L.L.C. Mr. Culp has written numerous articles on tax matters and is coauthor of a book on estate planning and business valuations. He can be reached at 704-372-6322.

The Bypass Trust: 300 to 1 on Your Money

Several years ago a couple in their midforties came to Bill for personal financial coaching. Because of a complication with one of their daughters, they'd had their 19-page will redrawn and asked Bill to review it. We don't review wills as neither of us is an attorney, but Bill wanted to know one thing. In all those pages of legalese, had they included a bypass trust? They said, "No. What's that?" He explained the concept and asked them to find out from their attorney why he hadn't recommend drawing one up.

Under federal estate law the total assets (regardless of how large) of the first spouse to die can go to the surviving spouse with no tax consequences. When the second spouse dies, $1 million is exempt from taxes in 2003. From there the exemption rises to $1.5 million per person in 2004 and 2005, leaps to $2 million in 2006–2008, and goes up to $3.5 million in 2009.

In 2010 the amount is unlimited. Because of the high and rising exemption limits, fewer than 2 percent of American families will pay federal estate taxes. However, if you and your family are in that 2 percent, this information is well worth knowing because federal tax rates start high beyond the exempted amount and quickly escalate to take away more than half your estate. When you take into account the value of your home, investments, retirement plans, potential inheritances, and life insurance proceeds, you could be worth a lot more than you think.

A bypass or credit-shelter trust allows up to $1,000,000 of the first spouse's assets to go around (bypass) the estate of the surviving spouse. The surviving spouse can get all the income from the trust and tap into the principal as well during his or her lifetime, but the real benefit is saving as much as $370,000 in federal taxes on $1 million when the second spouse passes away. That's $370,000 that will go to the children or grandchildren instead of to the tax collector, a gift from you to them.

Here's how it works. Let's say spouse A dies and leaves $1.2 million directly to spouse.B. There are no estate taxes. Let's say spouse B dies five years later and the estate has grown to $2 million. After the $1 million personal lifetime exemption is used, taxes must be paid on the remaining $1 million. Uncle Sam will take about $500,000; the couple's descendants will keep the other $500,000.

A better way is for spouse A to leave $200,000 to spouse B and put the remaining $1 million of assets into a bypass trust. If the assets in the trust appreciate to $2 million in five years, the entire amount will be free of taxes and be passed on to the children and/or grandchildren who will inherit the trust proceeds. Thus, a savings of $500,000 will be realized, not including state death taxes.

For roughly $1000 you can establish a bypass trust and rest assured that your heirs will receive a lot more money than they would without it. Even if your estate isn't all that large today, it could easily be a lot bigger than you think down the road.

To find out more, call your bank's trust officer. There's no charge for a consultation, and that officer can suggest a competent estate-planning attorney to help you. We emphasize "estate-planning attorney" because Bill's clients with the 19-page will didn't use one. If they hadn't visited Bill, they never would have known about that wonderful tax-saving device, the bypass trust.

The Perils of Joint Ownership

Joint ownership is a great way to avoid probate. Property automatically passes from one spouse to the other without having to go through court. But it does not reduce estate taxes as is often thought and in fact can raise them. Here's the reason.

If a couple owns their house jointly, one-half the total value of the house is included in the estate of the first spouse to die. That's no problem when the couple is married because the marital deduction means there is no estate tax.

The problem is that the house or other property is in the estate of the remaining spouse. If the estate is large enough, it will be fully taxed on that spouse's death.

Joint ownership often is considered a substitute for a will and other estate-planning tools. It's not. Here is a simple example of how it can work against you. Let's say a husband and wife jointly own a building worth $100,000 that's been depreciated to $10,000. If the building were sold, there'd be a $90,000 capital gain.

The husband dies. His half of the building passes to the wife on a "stepped-up basis." It's valued at $50,000, the market value on the date of his death. Shortly thereafter she sells the building for $100,000. Her cost is $55,000: $50,000 stepped up from the husband's half and one-half the depreciated value, $5000. That leaves a $45,000 taxable gain.

If the husband had sole title to the building, the stepped-up cost would be $100,000. Thus, when the wife sold it later for $100,000, there would be no taxes to pay.

According to PriceWaterhouse, "Couples often hold property jointly because one spouse—usually the wife—is concerned about her interest in the event of a divorce. This is understandable. However, almost all— if not all—states have now adopted the law of equitable property distribution upon divorce.

"Advice to put a home or any property solely in a husband's name can affect a wife's comfort level [or vice versa]. It is important for the couple to discuss the issues and determine whether the potential tax savings outweigh the emotional discomfort resulting from placing the property in one spouse's name alone."

Solo Retirement Plans

As was mentioned earlier, one-person 401(k)s (also known as individual or owner-only plans) may make a lot of sense for the self-employed since a 2001 change in the tax law. They offer a number of advantages compared to traditional plans such as Keoghs, SEPs, and Simple IRAs as long as the business has no more than one employee with a spouse.

The amount that can be contributed into a one-person 401(k) is $40,000 annually, more than double the maximum for certain other self-employed retirement plans. A worker can contribute as much as 25 percent of earnings plus the maximum $11,000 "elective deferral" as long as the $40,000 ceiling isn't exceeded. In general, this is an improvement for single employees whose annual income is no higher than $160,000 because more money can be set aside than can through other traditional retirement vehicles.

Here's a simple example of the benefits. Through a Simple IRA business owners making $100,000 annually could contribute $10,500 in 2002. With a SEP or Keogh, the maximum was $25,000, but with an owner-only 401(k) they could defer an additional $11,000 on top of the $25,000, a total of $36,000 each year; at age 50 and over it would be $37,000. That's $11,000 to $12,000 a year more than under any other plan.

At an annual income level of $50,000, the maximum you previously could contribute was $12,500. Now it's $23,500 or $24,500, depending on whether you are under 50. That works out to somewhere between 47 percent and 49 percent of your earnings. Very few people will be able to hit the maximum unless one spouse makes enough to take care of the family and the self-employed one can throw money into the 401(k).

Besides being able to invest more money, there are other advantages. For one thing, owners can make penalty-free loans to themselves and pay themselves interest as well. Most traditional retirement plans don't have that feature. But there is a caveat. If you borrow the money and are unable to repay it within the specified time frame, usually no more than five years, you not only will be socked with an early withdrawal penalty of 10 percent of the amount borrowed but will be taxed on the full amount withdrawn at ordinary tax rates.

Although solo 401(k)s have been around for quite a while, it wasn't until recently that financial firms actually tried to sell them because the administrative costs for participants were outrageous. Now, with the advent of technology and simplified tax rules, a company such as the John Hancock group of funds charges only $150 a year. Raymond James Financial will set up a plan for you for just $35 to start and $75 a year to maintain. The big plus is that you can buy individual stocks through Raymond James and not have to rely on mutual funds.

Just as in a regular 401(k), the solo versions are protected from creditors and bankruptcy claims under the federal Employee Retirement Income Security Act (ERISA). Another benefit is that it may be possible to roll over your other retirement plans to launch yours. Rollovers help cut the annual cost of the plan and also increase the size of the loan you could take out, assuming of course you decided to do that. Our advice on taking out a loan: Be very careful.

If you plan to expand your company beyond you, the 401(k) has to be available to all the employees. Whether they contribute and how much they contribute will affect your contribution limits as well. We suggest setting up a solo 401(k) only if you're sure you can manage your business with one employee only, that employee being you. Otherwise you may end up fighting the IRS, and you do not want to do that.

If You're a Small Business Owner, You Can Get a Special Estate-Tax Break

Nobody likes to think about or talk about death, but we don't know anyone who wants to give Uncle Sam more money after he or she passes away. Estate planning has to occur while you're alive, and now's as good a time as any to think about saving tax dollars.

If you don't own a business, this won't apply. But if you do, here's a tax angle few people know. Whenever a farm or a closely held business accounts for more than 35 percent of the gross estate's value, the estate is allowed to pay taxes for up to 14 years. In the initial five years only interest payments are required. Annual payments including interest then are made in the subsequent 9 years.

If a farm alone makes up more than 35 percent of the gross estate, sometimes those assets don't have to be valued at fair market value as would the assets of a closely held business. Let's assume the farm in question is worth $300,000 as an ongoing farm but $600,000 to a commercial developer. If the farm is valued at the higher figure, the tax burden on the survivors will be far greater.

If you comply with the "special use valuation," a complex part of the law, the farm can be valued for what it's worth if it were in theory to remain a farm even though the farm is likely to be sold for a different use after the estate is settled.

For additional background, check with an attorney who specializes in estate planning. If you don't know one, ask a trust officer where you bank. The advice is free and worth taking advantage of.

What Do You Do When You Know Your Spouse Is Going to Die?

This list can help during a very stressful time.

1. Call your lawyer.

2. Call your bank trust officer and/or investment adviser.

3. Go to your safety deposit box. The bank will seal it as soon as the obituary appears in the papers. Everything in the box will be taxed as if it belonged to your spouse's estate unless it is labeled with the owner's name or the true owner can prove ownership.

4. Set funeral plans in motion with your minister.

5. Call the funeral director.

6. You may want to suggest a charitable organization for a memorial fund instead of flowers.

7. Contact family members and close friends who live out of town. Remember the people around you; they also need to express their grief.

8. Make sure money is deposited in your account. Make sure salary continuation checks are made payable to your account and are available for immediate use.

9. Gather all personal papers: wills, insurance papers, property, and bills. All bills incurred before the death come out of the estate money for tax purposes. Keep a record of what you spend so that you can be reimbursed.

10. Cancel all credit cards in your spouse's name and have the cards you wish to keep reinstated in your name. Also, add your name as a guardian of any stock and make sure both spouses' names are listed as beneficiaries of any insurance policies for the children.

11. Have acknowledgment cards printed. This will save time when you need to thank people and are still grieving. Ask close friends to help you. On some cards you will want to write a note. Try to do this within three to four weeks.

12. Change your hospitalization plan from group to family. You have only one month to do this or you may lose the insurance.

13. Contact the local Social Security office and present military records and discharge papers (if any), your marriage certificate, and Social Security numbers for all family members. Don't trust the postal service with these important papers. You'll receive monthly Social Security checks for you and your children that can be deposited into your bank account automatically. When a child reaches age 18 years, he or she must let Social Security know about any plans to continue his or her education. If the plans are to continue, he or she will receive a monthly Social Security check; if not, the money is withdrawn and the amount is divided among the other children (if any) and you. If a child goes back to school later as a full-time student, he or she can be reinstated in the Social Security plan. You'll also receive a lump-sum death amount that can be sent directly to the funeral director and applied to his or her bill.

14. You might have trouble canceling some subscriptions or book club memberships in your spouse's name. Remember, you're not responsible for any literature or merchandise delivered to you once you have notified the companies. Your trust officer can cancel subscriptions. Always work in duplicate so that you'll have a record.

15. Update your own will and estate plan. Make sure your children's guardians are the best for the job. If you have a

responsible older child or family member, let that person know where you keep important papers. Your lawyer should have a copy of the will and the estate plan. Don't put them into the safety deposit box.

16. Have your lawyer check when the next income tax payment is due.

17. The bank may send an appraiser to your house to place a value on all your personal property for tax purposes. Yes, you will pay taxes on it again unless you can prove that the items do not belong to your spouse's estate.

18. Develop a "pat" answer for all the salespeople and financial advisers you'll hear from, such as "Call my trust officer or attorney with whom I must consult."

19. Write out your wishes about your own funeral and place it in your funeral director's files. This will spare your family and the children much pain.

20. When going through papers, look for all receipts the deceased may have for antiques, art, jewelry, stocks, bonds, property, furniture or other possessions, canceled checks, bill of sale, or any other evidence to establish what the deceased paid for. Also look for birth certificates, military records and discharge papers, Social Security numbers, your marriage certificate, insurance policies, savings bonds, wills, safety deposit boxes, evidence of indebtedness, records of employee benefits and contracts, and deeds or other evidence of property or corporation ownership. It is best to know where all these are in advance.

Once you've done this it's time to take care of yourself and your family. Let your lawyer and executor start to probate the will.

Eventually you'll have to assess your needs and decide where to proceed. Even if you have an adviser, at some point you must know what your estate and money are doing. Always make sure you have the option to remove your trust officer and/or investment adviser and choose another one or handle your own affairs.

The goal of estate planning is to (1) get as much of your and your family's assets where you'd like them to go by the time (2) you'd like them to be there and to (3) pay Uncle Sam and the state where you live as little in taxes as legally possible. As with so many financial decisions, the earlier you start, the more likely the success of your outcome and the less money and time it's likely to take. Remember, if Sam Walton could save at least $11 billion in taxes through early and proper estate planning—and have his assets end up where he wanted them to go—you and your family can do the same, albeit on a much smaller scale.

8

Seize Your Opportunities

I seen my opportunities and I took'em.
—COMMODORE VANDERBILT

 We've shared with you the secrets you need for living a full and wealthy life. Now we'll let the greatest sports coach of all take over.

Michael Jordan and Bill have at least two things in common. They are (1) graduates of the University of North Carolina and (2) had the pleasure (make that honor) to be there with Dean Smith, the winningest basketball coach in history, a class act of a human being, and a record setter without peer: 879 collegiate wins, 27 consecutive 20-win seasons (21 with at least 25 victories), 21 visits to the "Sweet Sixteen," 15 trips to the Final Eight, 11 trips to the Final Four, two NCAA championships, one NIT title, 13 ACC tournament crowns, one Olympic title, 224 lettermen, 52 players who turned pro, a 97.3 percent graduation rate—and Michael Jordan.

The Dean stunned sports fans around the world by opening a news conference in October 1997 with five chilling words: "I have decided to resign." Why are we telling you this? Because there are important lessons we can all learn from this man of principle that apply not only to investing but also to life, which is a heck of a lot more important than money.

1. A disciplined person is free.
2. There's a purpose to everything.
3. Unselfishness is a virtue.

4. Everything is scheduled, so it's important to be on time.
5. When Coach Smith (aka the market and economy) speaks, everyone listens.
6. Details and defense are priorities.
7. Teamwork is essential.

How do these principles apply to you and your family and to all of us in making money?

Discipline. To be disciplined means to be trained. You can't be successful as an investor unless you know the right things to do and the harmful things to avoid.

Purpose. There is a bigger purpose to making money than just having lots of it. Spending on necessities is one purpose. Giving to those who need it is another. Having some fun with your money is still another.

Unselfishness. One reason some people continually lose money is they aren't unselfish; they are the opposite: greedy. They want far more from their money than they should reasonably expect.

Scheduling and being on time. Having a regular time to review your and your family's finances and scheduling how often you're going to add to your portfolios will make you and all the members of your family wiser, more successful investors.

Listening. When Dean Smith spoke, his players listened because what he knew was worth knowing. Listening to what you and your family really want your money to do is important. Making money is one thing, and that's easy when you know what to do. But knowing why you want to make it and what you intend to do with it is even more critical.

Details and defense. The first step in making money is wasting less and saving more. If there's nothing saved, there's nothing to invest. The second step is not losing it, and that's where details come in. Keep up with your investments to see how they're performing and to ensure that they're doing what you and all your family members want. Make sure none of you is doing anything speculative. If you are, stop doing it.

Teamwork. Everyone needs help. We are your money coaches and hope to always be by continuing to earn your trust. You may also need others, such as a superior CPA and tax adviser. That person can help you save each year on taxes and preserve your estate so that it goes where you want it to go. Professional consultants can be worth many times the money they charge. And if they're not, fire them!

Our Ideas Really Do Work for Everyone

Let us share our enthusiasm about 18 students just outside St. Louis (Greenville, Illinois) who are from severely disadvantaged backgrounds (their families are at poverty level) but who now proudly own shares of Wal-Mart. Each of the 18 kids bought at least one share, and many siblings and parents kicked in a few dollars to become shareowners as well. Not only that, buying that one single share of stock was enough for some of these young people to turn their lives around. They dressed better. They paid closer attention in class. Their grades improved. Their self-esteem rose dramatically.

What is most remarkable about this story is that we had never met any of these young people. They were using our old guidebook called *How to Become a MultiMillionaire on Just $50 a Month*, and Bill worked with them on the telephone.

Our friend Don Clair, who ran a revolutionary prison-reform program at a federal correctional institution in Greenville, introduced us to this high school class. Don invited Bill to come out and coach not only the inmates but also the warden and the staff in addition to working with the inmates' spouses. Don's mission in life has always been helping the downtrodden. He's a master at turning negatives into positives. Bill was delighted to be able to contribute.

MARY ON MONEY

Mary collects stories of everyday people who live quiet lives but through sound investing have amassed fortunes that have benefited many people. One of her favorites is about Donald Othmer, a professor of chemical engineering in Brooklyn, and his wife, Mildred, a former teacher and buyer for her mother's dress store.

After they died in their nineties, friends and family members were shocked to learn that their combined estates were worth over $800 million and that they had given nearly everything to charity. How did they get so rich?

Very much like Herbert H. Goodman of Bremerton, Washington. For more than 50 years Goodman was a janitor and food-service worker at the Puget Sound Naval Shipyard. When he died at age 90, his estate was valued at $3 million.

Both the Othmers and Goodman years ago started buying blue-chip stocks. In the early 1960s the Othmers had the good fortune to turn over $50,000 to a relatively unknown money manager but an old family friend, Warren of Omaha. "They just rode along," he told the *New York Times*. "The investment never changed their lives."

In 1970 the Othmers received stock in Warren's new company, Berkshire-Hathaway, which owns many of *America's Finest Companies®*, including Gillette and Coca-Cola. The stock was trading at 42 then.

BANK ON IT

I DO NOT HAVE THE ABILITY TO GUESS THE UPS AND DOWNS OF THE STOCK MARKET AVERAGES OR THE TRENDS IN INDIVIDUAL STOCKS. MOST FORTUNES ARE BUILT ON OWNERSHIP OF SUCCESSFUL BUSINESS ENTERPRISES OVER A LONG PERIOD OF TIME.

T. Rowe Price

It's 72,000 now (and has been as high as 84,000). Mildred Othmer's 7500 shares alone are worth $525 million. Donald's, which were sold on his death when the price was lower, were worth only $210 million.

The Othmers were smart or lucky or both to ask Warren Buffet to manage their money, but that's not the lesson of this story. Even if they had simply put their money into the broad market, they would have ended up with between $50 million and $100 million.

BE READY FOR SUCCESS

We received this piece from Nightingale-Conant. Put these ideas to work for you and they will make a major difference in your life!

The Strangest Secret
"Our Changing World" Radio Transcript
by Earl Nightingale

When we say "nearly five percent of men and women achieve success" then we have to define success. The following is the best definition we've found: "Success is the progressive realization of a worthy ideal."

If a person is working toward a predetermined goal (we prefer the word "dream" instead) and knows where to go, then that person is successful. If a person does not know which direction they want to go in life, then that person is a failure.

"Success is the progressive realization of a worthy ideal."

Therefore, who succeeds?

The only person who succeeds is the person who is progressively realizing a worthy ideal. The person who says, "I'm going to become this" . . . and then begins to work toward becoming it.

Have you ever wondered why so many men and women work so hard and honestly without ever achieving anything in particular? Why others do not seem to work hard at all and yet get everything? We sometimes think it is the magic touch or pure luck. We often say, "Everything they touch turns to gold."

(continued)

Have you ever noticed that a person who becomes successful tends to continue this pattern of success? Or on the other hand, how a person who fails seems to continually fail?

Well, the answer is simple—those who succeed have established personal goals.

Success is not the result of making money; making money is the result of success and success is in direct proportion to our service.

Here are five steps that will help you realize success:

1. Establish a definite goal (dream is even better).

2. Stop running yourself down.

3. Do not think of all the reasons why you cannot be successful—instead think of all the reasons why you can achieve success.

4. Trace your emotions back to childhood—discover where you first got the negative idea you would not be successful—face your fears.

5. Renew your self-image by writing a description of the person you want to become—Act the part—you are that person!

George Bernard Shaw said:

"People are always blaming their circumstances for what they are. I don't believe in circumstances. The people who get on in this world are the people who get up and look for the circumstances they want, and if they can't find them, make them."

Well, that is pretty apparent, isn't it? And every person who discovered this believed—for a while—that he was the first one to work it out. We become what we think about.

Now, it stands to reason that a person who is thinking about a concrete and worthwhile goal is going to reach it, because that's what he's thinking about. And we become what we think about.

(continued)

Conversely, the man who doesn't know where he's going, and whose thoughts must therefore be thoughts of confusion and anxiety and fear and worry, becomes what he thinks about. His life becomes one of frustration and fear and anxiety and worry. And if he thinks about nothing . . . he becomes nothing.

So decide now. What is it you want? Plant your goal in your mind. It's the most important decision you'll ever make in your entire life. All you've got to do is plant that seed in your mind, care for it, and work steadily toward your goal, and it will become a reality.

How do you begin?

First: It is understanding emotionally as well as intellectually that we literally become what we think about; that we must control our thoughts if we're to control our lives. It's understanding fully that . . . "as ye sow, so shall ye reap."

Second: It's cutting away all fetters from the mind and permitting it to soar as it was divinely designed to do. It's the realization that your limitations are self-imposed and that the opportunities for you today are enormous beyond belief. It's rising above narrow-minded pettiness and prejudice.

Third: It's using all your courage to force yourself to think positively on your own problems, to set a definite and clearly defined goal for yourself. To let your marvelous mind think about your goal from all possible angles; to let your imagination speculate freely upon many different possible solutions. To refuse to believe that there are any circumstances sufficiently strong to defeat you in the accomplishment of your purpose. To act promptly and decisively when your course is clear. And to keep constantly aware of the fact that you are, at this moment, standing in the middle of your own "acres of diamonds."

And fourth: Save at least 10 percent of every dollar you earn.

It's also remembering that, no matter what your present job, it has enormous possibilities—if you're willing to pay the price by keeping these four points in mind:

(continued)

1. You will become what you think about.

2. Remember the word "imagination" and let your mind begin to soar.

3. Courageously concentrate on your goal [dream] every day.

4. Save 10 percent of what you earn.

Finally, take action—ideas are worthless unless we act on them.

We, Mary and Bill, are delighted to have had the privilege and honor of writing *Worry-Free Family Finances* for McGraw-Hill. They are genuinely nice people to work with and have supported our ideas for reaching you and your family, and we thank them.

With thousands of money and investing books in the marketplace, we have tried to make *Worry-Free Family Finances* stand out as the only investment book you and your entire family can enjoy. It is based on just six words: save more, give more, invest wisely.

Those six simple words form the foundation of a solid moneymaking program for you and your family that can take small amounts of money and turn it into a small fortune if not a large one. In addition, they remove the stress from personal and family finances.

Sean O'Casey wisely observed, "Money doesn't make you happy, but it quiets the nerves." We wholeheartedly agree. Live wealthy!

Wow! For the first time, the whole thing makes sense.
—Milo Bloom

FINANCIAL EDUCATION ON THE WEB

http://www.plan.ml.com/family/kids/. This Merrill Lynch website for young people lists books and other sites that teach about investing.

The public may boo me, but when I go home and think of my money I clap.

HORACE (EPISTLES, C. 20 BC)

http://www.salomonsmithbarney.com/yin/home.htm. Securities firm Salomon Smith Barney features materials for teaching financial literacy to young people.

http://www.nyse.com/about/education/outreach.html. Explanation of programs the New York Stock Exchange conducts for schoolteachers.

http://www.smg2000.org. Description of the *Stock Market Game,* an online learning tool for the classroom.

http://www.life-line.org. Explanations of life and health insurance.

http://personalfinance.firstunion.com. Tools and calculators for financial and retirement planning from Wachovia Corp.

http://www.myciti.com/calculators. Calculators for auto loans, life insurance, home financing and credit cards, and planners from Citibank.

Www.interest.com/hugh/calc. Offers a wide variety of easy-to-use calculators for uses ranging from retirement plans to mortgages.

http://www.calfed-edgate.com/visa. The "Get-Out-of-Debt Quiz Show" starts players out with $10,000 of debt. The right answers to questions get them out of debt.

http://www.fleetkids.com/fleet/home.b.html. The Fleet Bank site for children includes games and other activities.

http://www.sec.gov/investor/tools.shtml. The Securities and Exchange Commission's site has a "Test Your Money Smarts" interactive quiz for beginning investors.

9

Wow!

If there's one thing in your home, we bet it's a can of WD-40. According to a recent survey, more than 80 percent of U.S. households own at least one. Someone once described it as a cult product, and with that we agree. You can do multiple things with this simple little yellow-and-blue can: clean crayon marks from walls, shine the leaves of artificial plants, remove snarls from horsehair and manes, and restore the transparency of plastic shoes, assuming you own any.

For this reason we suggest that you check out www.wd40.com to learn more about how useful this singular product is and to sign up for its fun weekly newsletter. By the way, WD-40 was invented by NASA decades ago. The WD stands for "water dispersant." Forty means it was the fortieth concoction they came up with that did the job.

Here is a true story from one of our newsletter subscribers:

I was playing golf years ago with a doctor (MD) and swung a little too hard. My elbow became sore and began to hurt. My Dr. friend whipped out his can of W-D 40 and says "just where does it hurt" . . . sprayed some on and I declare, it got better. Be sure to carry a can in your golf bag. On questioning him about how helpful it really was, he told me a story. . . . Seems this patient of his was in pretty good health until 6 months after he retired. . . . Went to Dr. complaining of his joints hurting. . . . Dr. questioned him a little about his prior employment before retiring, and found out that he was a mechanic. . . . "Did you ever use WD 40?" was the question, "All the time." the patient said. . . . Well, you were absorbing it thru your work when you used it on those cars. . . . So just spray a little on each joint and give it time to do its job and you should be OK. Man never came back with joint problems after that. Oh, that was Dr. Bill Eckbert from Belmont. . . . Probably still plays golf in his 80s or early 90s. Gotta go. Best regards, Whit

STILL HAVEN'T DONE ALL YOUR CHRISTMAS SHOPPING?

Whether you're shopping for holidays gifts or at any other time of year, you might want to check out www.eDealFinder.com. You could uncover discounts up to 50 percent and more off at hundreds of online stores from Amazon.com to The Sharper Image. You can ferret out deals by store, product, category, or the amount you wish to save. This is a very easy, well-laid-out site, even for computer nonnerds like us.

And while you're at it, take a look at www.eDealinfo.com as well. Both sites offer free e-mail newsletters.

BIZ ACTIONS LLC

We've been getting a free weekly newsletter from Biz Actions LLC for a number of months. A recent issue covered the monetary benefits of giving to charity by reducing taxes through such actions as giving away appreciated securities instead of cash, donating a used car to your favorite charity, avoiding the tax trap of gifts of art, writing off expenses for doing volunteer work, and the types of records you need in case the IRS comes calling. We would encourage you to log on to www.bizactions.com and check it out—a lot of fine information at no charge.

A TRUE HORROR STORY ABOUT PERSONAL FRAUD

We've all heard horror stories about fraud that's committed using your name, address, Social Security number, credit, and so on. Unfortunately I (author of this piece, a friend of the Statons) have firsthand knowledge because my wallet was stolen last month. Within a week the thieve(s) ordered an expensive monthly cell-phone package, applied for a VISA credit card, had a credit line approved to buy a Gateway computer, and received a PIN number from the DMV to change my driving record information online. And more.

Here's some critical information to limit the damage in case this happens to you or someone you know. As everyone always advises, cancel your credit cards immediately. The key is having the toll-free numbers and your card numbers handy so you know whom to call. Keep those where you can find them easily (having to hunt for them is additional stress you *won't* need at that point)!

File a police report immediately in the jurisdiction where the card(s) was stolen. This proves to credit providers you were diligent and is a first step toward an investigation (if there ever is one). But here's what is perhaps most important—call the three national credit reporting organizations immediately to place a fraud alert on your name and Social Security number.

I had never heard of doing this until advised by a bank that called to tell me an application for credit was made over the Internet in my name. The alert means any company that checks your credit knows your information was stolen, and they have to contact you by phone to authorize new credit.

By the time I was advised to do this—almost 2 weeks after the theft—all the damage had been done (there are records of all the credit checks initiated by the thieves' purchases, none of which I knew about before placing the alert). Since then, no additional damage has been done, and the thieves threw my wallet away this weekend (someone turned it in). It seems to have stopped them in their tracks.

Key phone numbers are:

Equifax 1-800 525-6285
Experian (formerly TRW) 1-800-301-7195
Trans Union 1-800-680-7289
The Social Security Administration also has a fraud line at
1-800-269-0271.

SLOW DOWN ON YOUR PHONE NUMBER

We don't know about you, but we get sick and tired of people calling and rattling off their phone numbers so quickly that even a computer couldn't take them down. So we're fighting back, in a friendly manner of course.

We no longer listen and relisten to messages to try to pick up a garbled phone number. Period! It is an insult to all of us to have to put up with people who want a phone call returned but aren't courteous enough to give us time to write it down.

If it's really important, the party will call back. If it's not, the message was probably not worth hearing in the first place.

So when you want a phone call returned, slow down and give the number to the other party so that it can be put on paper. Then repeat the number. It's a simple matter of courtesy. You're sure to score 100 percent on returned calls you really want to have returned.

FOR YOUR HEALTH

We get a free entertaining and useful newsletter on health you might want to check out. Log on to www.hsibaltimore.com and try it. If you don't like it, please let us know.

E-BROCHURES TO TAKE YOU THERE

Log on to www.travelbooksusa.com and get the free e-brochures they offer at no charge on more than 220 of America's most scenic drives. Included in each brochure are details about vehicle limitations if there are any, best travel seasons, campgrounds, things to do and see, and nearby parks and national forests. It's good stuff and won't cost you a penny.

IF YOU HAVE AN AUTO ACCIDENT

A website you might want to check is www.insure.com. Life can get very complicated in the aftermath of a car accident. Questions about injuries, car repairs, talking to the police, and filing an insurance claim— not to mention the scare-induced adrenaline rush—bombard your senses and can leave you incapable of making a clear decision.

The first thing to do at the crash site is to determine the extent of driver and passenger injuries. If the accident is a fender bender, emergency medical care may not be necessary. However, when in doubt, call an ambulance.

If your first phone call was to emergency care providers, your second call should be to the police. The police will tell you whether it's required to move the crashed vehicles from moving traffic, and an investigating officer will take statements from the drivers and passengers involved. Even if the facts of the accident are embarrassing or detrimental to you, tell the truth. If you alter your story down the road or don't disclose pertinent facts, the insurance companies involved will find out. That could come back to haunt you; the insurer can deny coverage or shift more fault to you.

It's not your place to accuse another party of being at fault, so limit the statement to the facts. By the same token, you should avoid saying "I'm sorry" because that can be interpreted as an admission of fault.

Make sure to exchange insurance information with the other drivers involved. If another driver gives you an insurance ID card, check its date to make sure the coverage is in force. In addition, get the names and phone numbers of witnesses. Although it's not your job to investigate the accident, getting witness contact information can make the insurer's and investigating officer's jobs easier.

You also should get the investigating officer's contact information for future reference. The officer's report is not available at the accident scene.

Your auto insurance policy requires you to inform your insurer when you've been involved in an accident. As soon as you are able, you must call your insurer and file an accident report. You also should notify the other driver's insurer of the accident. The insurance companies involved then will begin an investigation of the accident to determine who was at fault.

A good way to notify your insurer is by calling your agent, especially if the accident is minor. Agents often have the authority to settle minor property-damage claims (below $5000) by issuing a check to you. However, if the accident involves injuries and major property damage and you are insured by a company that employs "exclusive" agents, don't expect your agent to lobby the claims adjuster on your behalf. Exclusive agents sell policies for one insurer only and are forbidden from interfering in the claims process.

Independent agents are a different story. They often are able to "go to bat" for you with the insurance company's claims adjuster because insurers more and more are looking to independent agents to sell their products and are not interested in souring a relationship with an independent agent over one claim.

It's imperative to ask the insurance company adjuster for a copy of the complete claim file—Post-it notes and all—because increasingly, insurers are destroying documents in an effort to move to a "paperless office." Insurers make mistakes from time to time, and it's possible that you could be surcharged for an accident even though it wasn't your fault. If you don't have a copy of the claim file, it's unlikely that your insurer will have the documents by the time you catch the surcharge, sometimes weeks or months after the accident.

Insurers aren't keen on giving out copies of claim files. If the insurer doesn't give you a copy, file a complaint with your state's department of insurance and contact a lawyer. The lawyer probably will have to subpoena the insurer to produce a copy of the claim file before the insurer gives it to you.

You have every right to seek what you deem appropriate medical care. An auto insurer cannot direct you to a certain medical care provider unless you've signed for a preferred provider organization discount. Keep in mind, however, that embellishing your medical bills or seeking unnecessary treatment raises red flags for insurers: Be prepared for a letter from the insurer saying that it won't pay all the medical expenses if you've sought extensive treatment for a minor injury.

In addition, don't give up your right to choose an auto-repair facility. Finding a repair shop that performs quality work independent of insurers can save you the hassle of haggling over repairs or procedures not performed at insurance company direct-repair shops (DRP). While many DRPs no doubt perform quality repairs, they sign agreements with insurers to give discounts on parts, labor, and procedures in exchange for a steady stream of crashed cars. In short, the DRP may not be acting in your best interest.

Hiring a lawyer is not required after you've crashed into someone, but there are a couple of scenarios in which seeking legal counsel is a good idea. If you've been injured seriously in the accident, you'll probably want a lawyer to help keep the lines of communication open between you and the insurance company and help you receive a fair settlement.

Proving to another driver's insurer that its policyholder caused the accident might require the services of an attorney as well. To prove the other driver is at fault, you have to show what the rules of the road are in the accident scenario, prove that the other driver disobeyed the rules of the road, prove that the driver's disobedience caused the accident, and that the accident caused harm to you or damage to your car. That might seem simple, but it requires substantial time, research, and knowledge of the law.

If you live in a no-fault state and have been injured in an accident, you will make your claim under your own auto insurance policy for reimbursement of medical expenses and lost wages. However, in most no-fault states you still can make a claim for damages to your car under the at-fault party's insurance.

One other situation that should send you to a lawyer's office is when you have not been able to collect any insurance benefits within 30 days of the accident. That's a signal of big trouble: Either the insurer is getting ready to litigate against you or you have not communicated effectively with the insurer. In both cases an attorney is helpful.

The critical points to remember to ensure a smooth insurance claim after an accident are as follows:

1. Be honest with your insurer and the other insurers involved even if the facts of the accident seem to weigh against you.

2. Know where you are going for medical treatment and car repairs.

3. Obtain as many documents as possible to avoid surcharges or problems getting insurance in the future.

LOW-TECH VIRUS PROTECTION

One of Bill's fellow faculty members at Mentor University (online and live seminars and personal/corporate training; http://www.mentoru. com/staton) shared this idea for not spreading e-mail viruses to others in your computer's address book. It comes courtesy of the TEAMOS/2 Technical Support List. The author, Mike Kilroy, is a knowledgeable individual.

To avoid spreading computer viruses, create a contact in your email address book with the name !0000 with no email address in the details.

This contact will then show up as your first contact. If a virus attempts to do a "send all" on your contact list, your pc will put up an error message saying: "The Message could not be sent. One or more recipients do not have an e-mail address. Please check your Address Book and make sure all the recipients have a valid e-mail address."

You click on OK and the offending (virus) message would not have been sent to anyone. Of course, make no changes to your original contacts list. The offending (virus) message may then be moved to your "Drafts" or "Outbox" folder. Go there and delete the offending message. Problem is solved and virus is not spread.

Try this and pass it on to your email contacts.

PAY OFF YOUR MORTGAGE EARLY?

If you absolutely, positively cannot live with a mortgage of any size at any rate of interest, then by all means pay it off. Otherwise, that might not be a sound investment decision. Here's why.

In our weekly *E-Money Digest* (http://www.billstaton.com/products. htm), Bill runs a "Guided Portfolio" that's up about 78 percent since mid-June 2000 (26 percent a year annualized), a period in which the market has been off as much as the portfolio has been up. In this week's issue, the current yield is 5.6 percent, so let's use that yield to make our point.

Let's say you come into a lump sum and want to pay down your current 30-year mortgage with a 6.5 percent interest rate. Part of that interest is tax-deductible. Let's assume your tax bracket is 33 percent. Thirty-three percent of 6.5 percent is 2.17 percent, and so your real interest cost after taxes is just 4.33 percent (6.5 percent −2.17 percent). That's the amount you in essence earn by paying the debt down.

Now, instead of putting that $100,000 against your mortgage, let's say you invest it in the Guided Portfolio with a starting (and growing) yield of 5.6 percent. After you pay taxes on that income at 33 percent, your net return is 3.73 percent, which is less than your net mortgage payment. If that's all you got from the portfolio over the next 30 years, then it would be better to start paying it down since 4.33 percent is a better return than 3.73 percent.

But we invest in *America's Finest Companies*®, which raise their dividends each year. Therefore, the income stream, both before and after taxes, is going to rise annually. In addition, you surely will make some capital gains, most of which will be long-term and taxed at a 15 percent rate. Based on our above-average record of beating the market with below-market risk, we believe you can earn at around 9 percent a year. If that is true, 5.6 percent of that would come from dividends, and the other 3.4 percent from capital gains taxed at 15 percent (for a net 2.72 percent from the gains). Net dividends of 3.73 percent coupled with net gains of 2.72 percent add up to a 6.45 percent annual return after taxes, significantly higher than the savings of 4.33 percent a year on your mortgage.

Pay off your mortgage early if you want to, but unless you're a total dunderhead managing your money, it probably won't be a good deal because 4.33 percent a year for 30 years on $100,000 grows to $356,678. At 6.45 percent a year, it rises to $652,184, versus $295,506. Which would you rather have?

GIFT CERTIFICATES DO EXPIRE, AND YES, IT'S LEGAL IN MOST STATES

Zany Brainy will deduct a "service fee" for using a card more than one year old and also reduce the value of the card month by month until it hits zero. Consumers usually are stunned to find out that their gift certificates and gift cards can and do lose value. Barnes & Noble's gift cards read, "After 18 months of nonuse, a $1.50 per month dormant account fee will be charged, except where prohibited by law." Borders book chain warns that its cards are worthless after 24 months.

So what must you do? Make sure you don't let your gift cards/certificates lose their value. Read their terms and adhere to them.

CREDIT CARDS ARE VERY COSTLY

We always knew credit cards were costly, but recently we received confirmation from Consumers Union. Based on an annual 17 percent interest rate (rates are often higher and can and do run as much as 30 percent per year), a $5000 card balance will take 40 years and 2 months to pay off at a total cost of $16,305 (this assumes the cardholder pays a minimum of 2 percent of the balance or $10 a month, whichever is greater). If you have credit-card balances, pay them off as soon as possible and switch to a debit card.

WHAT WOULD YOU DO IF YOU LOST YOUR WALLET?

We went to see a great movie, *Rabbit-Proof Fence*, one Saturday afternoon, and Bill's wallet fell out of his pocket, but he didn't realize it until the next day. Bill asked the theater manager to go back and check our seats, and fortunately, the wallet was stuck where no one else would see it. Thus, nothing was missing and there was nothing else to worry about, right?

Well, it worried both of us because we started to think about what would have happened had it disappeared. Did Bill know the entire contents? The answer was no.

In case something like this happens again, Bill will have an inventory of everything in his wallet and so will Mary. You see, each of us made copies of all credit cards, shopping cards, driver's license, insurance card, and so on, and filed them in a safe place. It would be a nuisance to replace all the contents, but at least now we know what would have to be replaced.

PROTECT YOUR VALUABLE PHOTOS

Bill is a serious amateur photographer, and so he is very picky about getting film safely home when he flies. With all the enhanced "security" at airports designed to make everyone at least "feel" safer, x-ray scanners are becoming more hazardous to your film. (We wish we knew what this was doing to our bodies. Anyone out there got a guess?)

Virtually every decent-sized U.S. airport now employs a new breed of powerful scanner that can wipe out your film whether it's been exposed or not. Of course, they say they're looking for explosives, but meanwhile they're destroying your film, which not only is costly in a monetary sense but is a huge loss if you have some really good shots from a family reunion in France.

Here's what you need to know. A Kodak expert says film packed in your check-ins "will be damaged," and he emphasizes that he's "not kidding." Even if the film is in the camera, same outcome.

Film carried onto the plane, at least in the United States, stands a much better chance of being undamaged if it's scanned fewer than five times. Carry-on x-rays are much less powerful than those for checked luggage, at least for the time being.

Under the law—and the United States is the only country where this is true—you have the legal right to insist that your film and camera be hand inspected, thus bypassing the scanner altogether. If the inspector fails to comply, don't give up. Demand to speak to a supervisor. This is your legal right, and a lot of these people simply don't know it because they are new to their jobs.

Digital cameras do not have this problem. Another option is to have film developed before you fly back, particularly overseas, where we can guarantee that all your stuff will go through powerful x-ray machines. Many pros buy film in each country they visit and send home the film via FedEx before they travel on elsewhere. To us, that's the best and safest option of all, although it is quite a bit more expensive.

Take lots of great photos wherever you travel and use this advice to make sure they come back home safely with you for all to share.

FOR BETTER HEALTH, CHECK OUT

Dr. Andrew Weil (www.DrWeil.com) is a best-selling author, medical doctor, and nutritional expert. We found his site more than a year ago and immediately signed up for his daily newsletter, which is both informative and entertaining, plus it's free. In addition, this man loves to cook—healthily, that is—and offers recipes that are easy to prepare and taste good too.

Our dentist said recently that good teeth and gums are one of the finest signs of a good heart and vascular system. He should know because it wasn't long ago that he was in the Cleveland Clinic getting a defective heart valve repaired, and that was one thing he learned.

In a recent newsletter, Dr. Weil spoke of the benefits of an enzyme called CoQ10; it is produced naturally, but as we all get older we end up with less and less of it. Not only does it strengthen the heart and circulatory system, it also helps the teeth and gums, especially the gums. Bill has been taking it for years, and we know that to be true. His gums started to get noticeably better. Bill takes 60 milligrams per day. Dr. Weil says a range of 60 to 100 mg is fine.

A CHECKUP FOR YOUR 401(K)

From almost out of nowhere, the 401(k) has become popular as companies shift the retirement burden from their backs to the backs of employees. Roughly 25 percent of private-pension assets are in 401(k)s.

According to a recent survey, about 80 percent of companies that sponsor plans have only a foggy grasp of how much their plans actually cost. These plans are sold as packages, and the packages are priced in so many different ways that it's hard for employers to get an apples-to-apples comparison between one plan and another. There are all sorts of expenses, including plan design, investment management, payroll deduction, record keeping, regulatory compliance, and communications with employees; also, many of the mutual funds charge sales loads.

These expenses, which can eat up as much as 3 percent of assets per year, may not be picked up 100 percent by employers. In most cases they're shared with participants; the company pays for record keeping and administration, and the employee pays for investment management. But that's not always the case and in the future probably will be less common.

Smaller companies tend to pass on all the costs to employees. Some bigger companies are now doing the same thing. That seems fair enough since the plan is for the employees' benefit, but there's a rub. Employees get no say-so about who administers their plan, which investment firms manage it, or which or how many investment options to offer. And virtually no employee knows the actual annual cost of his or her 401(k). Granted, he or she may know some of the costs, but the companies rarely uncover them all.

How much your plan costs you makes a major difference in how much money you need to set aside each year to reach your retirement goals. Here's an illustration. Employees A, B, and C put $4000 per year into the equity funds (we wish it were individual stocks of *America's Finest Companies®*) of their 401(k)s. The three funds compound at exactly the same rate—12 percent per year—over the next 20 years. It costs A 0.5 percent per year to be in his plan. B pays 1 percent, and C pays 1.5 percent.

At the end of two decades, A will accumulate $303,303, B will have $285,060, and C will end up with $267,988. That's $35,315—12 percent less than A even though C's return is the same. This example assumes no company match. With a match, expenses create an even larger dollar gap. Costs are critical. Every extra dollar you pay in costs is a dollar that won't earn anything.

What should you know about your 401(k)? Contact your company's benefits administrator and find out about the following:

1. Total annual costs including operating expenses and investment management fees

2. Whether the funds charge a front-end or back-end sales load and how much

3. The performance of the investment options you've chosen versus standard benchmarks such as the S&P 500

These are the three most important things you need to know. As a general rule, if you're paying more than 1 percent per year in total expenses, it's too much. If the mutual funds charge sales loads, that's a negative because there are plenty of no-load funds with records just as good. If your investment performance before expenses continuously lags the benchmarks, that's negative too.

Once you're fully armed with information, you're in a position to complain if you're dissatisfied. Will your complaints mean anything? There's no way to know in advance, but at least you can voice an intelligent opinion.

Even if no one listens, knowing the basics about your 401(k) will help you determine whether you need to contribute more annually to reach your retirement goal or, if you're already at the limit, whether to save for retirement outside the 401(k).

Some employers don't help nearly as much as they could or should. In the end the retirement burden rests on your shoulders, not theirs, and they know it, but even so 401(k)s and other retirement plans are still in general a super deal. It's a shame more Americans don't take maximum advantage of them or any advantage at all.

SHOULD YOU BE A GOLD BUG?

Here's a letter we received recently, followed by our answer.

Dear Statons,

I am constantly getting calls from brokers wanting me to join the gold club and start putting some money into hard assets, i.e., gold coins, numismatics, etc. Could you please address this in a Weekly on Wealth!?

Dear John,

The people trying to get you to buy these things probably know even less than you. They're trying to take advantage of a weak stock market and the fear a lot of people have about their financial futures. For your information, for 200 years the value of gold has failed to keep up with the cost of living. Why it makes sense now makes no sense to us.

As for coins and bills, that is a real specialty area. We have made a few spectacular buys, but that was because we went to authentic dealers who knew what they were doing. You don't buy "investment" coins, art, antiques, or any other specialty items over the phone from people you don't know and who don't know you. Period!!

Glossary of Common Investment Terms

Account executive
The title given by some brokerage firms to their stockbrokers. Other variations on the title include registered representative, financial counselor, and financial consultant.

After-tax proceeds
Money received from a sale after commissions, fees, taxes, and any other expenses have been deducted.

Annual report
This document contains information about the performance of a company or mutual fund. For a company, it contains a record of the company's financial condition, including earnings and operating expenses. For a fund, it shows the fund's performance, how it invests shareholders' money to achieve those results, what the fund is doing currently, and its future plans. It should also include performance charts that calculate returns for hypothetical investments and managers' analysis.

Annuity
A series of regular payments, usually from an insurance company, guaranteed to continue for a specific time, usually the annuitant's lifetime, in exchange for a single payment or a series of payments to the company.

Bearish
A bear thinks the market is going to go down. Bearish is the opposite of bullish.

Beneficiary
A person or organization designated to receive the funds or other property from an annuity, insurance policy, retirement account, trust, will, or other contract.

Blue chip
Describes stocks of companies known for high-quality management or products that have a long history of stable earnings and/or dividend growth.

Bond
An interest-bearing security that obligates the issuer to pay a specified amount of interest for a specified time, usually several years, and then repay the bondholder the face amount of the bond. Bonds issued by corporations are backed by corporate assets; in case of default, the bondholders have a legal claim on those assets. Bonds issued by government agencies may or may not be collateralized. Interest from corporate bonds is taxable; interest from municipal bonds, which are issued by state and local governments, is free of federal income taxes and, usually, the income taxes of the issuing jurisdiction. Interest from Treasury bonds, which are issued by the federal government, is free of state and local income taxes but subject to federal taxes.

Book value
The net asset value of a company, determined by subtracting its liabilities from its assets. Dividing the result by the number of shares of common stock issued by the company yields the book value per share, which can be used as a relative gauge of the stock's value.

Bullish
A bull is someone who thinks the market is going to go up; bullish is the opposite of bearish.

Capital gain
The difference in value between what you originally paid for an investment and the higher price at which it was sold; the opposite of a capital loss.

Cost basis

Cost basis is used to determine capital gains and losses. Generally, cost basis is the original price of a security, including commissions and applicable fees. There are special rules for determining the basis in some situations (i.e., property received by gift or bequest, as compensation, or in a tax-free exchange).

Current yield

The annual interest on a bond divided by the current market price or the annual cash dividend divided by the current price of a stock.

Custodial account

An account for the benefit of a minor with an adult as the custodian.

Defined-contribution plan

A company retirement plan such as a 401(k) or 403(b) in which the employee elects to defer salary into the plan and directs the investments of that deferral.

Dividend

A distribution of company earnings to shareholders. Dividends typically are paid in cash or stock. You may choose automatic dividend reinvestment to buy more shares.

Earnings

The amount of profit a company realizes over a given time period after all costs, expenses, and taxes have been paid.

Exchange

A marketplace or any organization or group that provides or maintains a marketplace for trading securities, options, futures, or commodities. Examples of exchanges are the New York Stock Exchange (NYSE) and the American Stock Exchange (AMEX).

Expense ratio

A mutual fund's cost of doing business passed on to shareholders; expressed as a percentage of assets.

Fixed-income securities
Debt securities or IOUs for borrowed money. They obligate the borrower to pay the owner interest during the term of the loan and to return the principal or face value when the loan matures. A variety of institutions issue debt obligations, including the U.S. government, state and local governments, publicly held companies, banks, and savings and loans.

Index
A statistical composite that measures changes in the economy or financial markets. Some indexes are used as benchmarks against which economic or financial performance is measured. Some well-known market indexes are the Standard & Poor's 500, Dow Jones Industrial Average, NASDAQ, consumer price index (CPI), and Russell 2000. Indexes cannot be invested in directly, are unmanaged, and do not incur management fees, costs, or expenses.

Individual retirement account (IRA)
A tax-deferred retirement account for individuals that allows them to earn potential income on their investments and defer the taxes until withdrawals begin. Those who meet certain participation and income qualifications can make deductible contributions to an IRA. (Such contributions qualify as a deduction against earned income.) All others can contribute on a nondeductible basis.

Investment objective
The outcome desired by an investor or a mutual fund. For example, "current income" and "capital appreciation" are types of investment objectives.

Keogh plan
A tax-deferred, qualified retirement account for self-employed persons and employees of unincorporated businesses. Contributions and earnings are deductible from gross income and grow tax-deferred until withdrawn (certain restrictions apply). Qualified plans meet the requirements of the Internal Revenue Code, making them eligible for favorable tax treatment.

Leverage
The degree to which a company or individual is using borrowed money.

Liabilities
The sum of all outstanding debts: what a company or individual owes its creditors.

Long-term capital gains
Gains from the sale or exchange of a capital asset held for more than one year (at least one year and one day from the purchase date). Long-term capital gains are taxed at more favorable rates than are short-term gains.

Long-term debt
Liabilities that are repayable after one year or longer.

Market capitalization
The total value of a company's stock.

Municipal bond
A bond issued by a state, municipality, or revenue district. Municipal bonds (also called "munis") are exempt from federal and, in some cases state and city taxes. Some investors in bonds or bond funds may be subject to the alternative minimum tax.

Mutual fund
An investment company that pools money from shareholders and invests in a variety of securities, including stocks, bonds, and money-market instruments. A mutual fund stands ready to buy back (redeem) its shares at their current net asset value, which depends on the total market value of the fund's investment portfolio at the time of redemption. As open-end investments, most mutual funds continuously offer new shares to investors.

Net income
For a business, total revenue minus total expenses; the same as its net profit or earnings.

No-load mutual fund
A mutual fund that has no sales charge when shares are bought or sold.

Operating expenses
The business expenses that mutual fund companies pass on to share-holders, including management fees and 12b-1 fees. These costs are paid from a fund's assets before earnings are distributed to shareholders.

Ordinary income
Income other than a capital gain. For example, ordinary income includes wages, dividends, and interest earned on savings.

Price/earnings (P/E) ratio
The price of a stock divided by earnings per share.

Profit-sharing plan
A plan that enables employers to share profits with employees, at the employer's discretion. The compensation may be stocks, bonds, or cash and can be immediate or deferred until retirement.

Prospectus
A legal document offering securities or mutual fund shares for sale. When you invest in a mutual fund, the prospectus will provide valu-able information about the specific goals, fees, and practices of the fund. Federal and state securities regulators require that the prospectus include the fund's investment objectives, policies and restrictions, and fees and expenses and how shares can be bought and sold. It should be read carefully before you invest.

Registered investment adviser (RIA)
An individual who is registered with the Securities and Exchange Com-mission (SEC) in accordance with the Investment Advisers Act of 1940. Advisors are required to register annually with the SEC and to disclose any potential conflicts of interest they have concerning recommenda-tions made for their clients.

Return
The change in the value of an investment over a given period of time, expressed as a percentage of the total amount invested (including reinvestment of any dividends and capital gains distributions).

Risk
The possibility of loss of some or all of the money you invest. Also, the degree of probability of such a loss.

Rollover IRA
A tax-free transfer of assets from one qualified retirement plan to another.

Roth IRA
A type of individual retirement account that allows retirement savings to grow tax-free. You pay taxes on contributions but not on withdrawals (subject to certain rules). To participate in a Roth IRA, taxpayers are subject to certain income limits.

S&P 500 (Standard & Poor's 500 Index)
Considered to be a benchmark of the overall U.S. stock market. This index is composed of 500 widely held blue chip stocks representing industrial, transportation, utility, and financial companies with a heavy emphasis on industrials.

Securities and Exchange Commission (SEC)
A government regulatory agency that oversees and enforces the securities laws of the United States, publishes rules and guidance for the securities industry, and provides investor education.

SEP IRA (Simplified Employee Pension IRA)
An individual retirement account set up by a small business employer or by a self-employed person provided that certain requirements are met and there is no 401(k) plan in place. A SEP IRA is funded by contributions from the employer for his or her own benefit and that of any employees.

Simple IRA (Savings Incentive Match Plan IRA)

A retirement plan for employees of companies that do not have a 401(k) plan and employ fewer than 100 people. A Simple IRA allows the employees to set aside a percentage of their pretax wages into a special individual retirement account. The employer is required to contribute to the employee's plan. Employer contributions may vary from year to year. All contributions and earnings grow tax-deferred until withdrawn.

Surrender charges

Fees for terminating a certificate of deposit (CD), insurance, or annuity contract before it matures.

Tax-deferred

A provision that allows taxes to be postponed until a later date. Generally this applies to investments in retirement plans, annuities, savings bonds, and employee stock option plans.

Time horizon

The amount of time, usually years, that you expect to keep an amount of money invested.

Total assets

The combined value of all items of monetary value owned by an individual or business. A company's assets include tangible assets such as equipment, inventory, and real property and intangible assets such as goodwill (the value of a company's name in the market), patents, and other intellectual property, which are owned by a company and given monetary value in the company's balance sheet.

Total revenue

Total of all sales and income generated by a company.

Trade confirmation

A written statement acknowledging a securities transaction and its details.

Traditional IRA
Another name for a standard individual retirement account. This name more clearly distinguishes it from other types of IRAs, such as a Roth IRA.

Treasury bill
A short-term debt security of the U.S. government, also known as a T-bill. T-bills usually are held for a short time period (i.e., three months to one year) and can be converted easily into cash. T-Bills typically are sold at a discount and are exempt from state and local taxes. The money you will make on a T-bill is the difference between the face value of the T-bill and what you paid for it. T-bills are sold in $1000 increments.

Treasury note
A midterm debt security of the U.S. government with maturities ranging from 2 to 10 years that pays a fixed rate of interest every six months and returns its face value at maturity. The minimum denomination is $5000 plus $1000 increments for a 2- to 3-year maturity, or $1000 plus $1000 for a 4- to 10-year maturity.

Treasury security
A debt obligation of the U.S. government that is issued through the Department of the Treasury. Since they are backed by the full faith and credit of the U. S. government, these securities are considered virtually free from risk of default. For individual investors, the income of Treasuries is exempt from state and local taxes.

Vested
The percentage of ownership in a retirement plan's assets.

Volatility
The magnitude and frequency of changes in a security's value within a short period. The more volatile an investment, the higher its risk and potential return. Volatility usually is measured by calculating the annualized standard deviation of the daily change in price.

Volume

The daily number of shares traded in a security.

Yield

The annual rate of return of an investment paid in dividends or interest, expressed as a percentage. For a mutual fund, the yield is the rate of return earned by the securities in the fund's portfolio, less the funds expenses during a specified period. A fund's yield is expressed as a percentage of the maximum offering price per share on a specified date.

12b-1 Fee

A fee charged by a mutual fund company to pay for marketing, advertising, and distribution services. The 12b-1 distribution fee ranges from 0.25 percent to 1.0 percent of the fund's assets.

401(k)

A type of salary deferral retirement plan that allows employees to make pretax contributions from earned income that reduce their taxable income. Employers can match some or all contributions subject to maximum.

403(b)

A qualified retirement plan similar to 401(k) plans designed for nonprofit organizations. Qualified plans meet the requirements of the Internal Revenue Code, making them eligible for favorable tax treatment.

457 plan

A qualified retirement plan for state employees and employeesss of certain tax-exempt organizations that allows them to make systematic pretax contributions to their individual retirement savings accounts. Contibutions in a 457 plan grow tax-deferred.

Index

About the Authors

Bill and **Mary Staton** are the founders of The Staton Institute, a family financial education and consulting center. They have been profiled in *The Wall Street Journal, Money, Barron's, BusinessWeek,* and other major publications.